CW00350661

79
ON THE RADIO

JOHN LUDDEN

Copyright© 2023 John Ludden

All rights reserved. No part of this book may be reproduced, stored in a retrieval system, or transmitted, in any form or by any means, electronic, mechanical, photocopying, recording or otherwise without permission in writing from the copyright owner.

A Special thanks to Paul Collier and all who have contributed with their stories of Wednesday 4ᵗʰ April 1979.

UK TOP FORTY ON 4ᵀᴴ APRIL 1979

1: BRIGHT EYES: ART GARFUNKEL
2: COOL FOR CATS: SQUEEZE
3: SOME GIRLS: RACEYRAK
4: IN THE NAVY: THE VILLAGE PEOPLE
5: I WILL SURVIVE: GLORIA GAYNOR
6: HE'S THE GREATEST DANCER: SISTER SLEDGE
7: SILLY THING/WHO KILLED BAMBI: SEX PISTOLS AND TEN POLE TUDOR
8: SULTANS OF SWING: DIRE STRAITS
9: SHAKE YOUR BODY (DOWN TO THE GROUND): THE JACKSONS
10: THE RUNNER: THE THREE DEGREES
11: SOMETHING ELSE/FRIGGIN' IN THE RIGGIN': THE SEX PISTOLS
12: I WANT YOUR LOVE: CHICA
13: TURN THE MUSIC UP: PLAYERS ASSOCIATION
14: WOW: KATE BUSH
15: STRANGE TOWN THE: JAM
16: DON'T STOP ME NOW: QUEEN
17: OLIVER'S ARMY: ELVIS COSTELLO AND THE ATTRACTIONS
18: MONEY IN MY POCKET: DENNIS BROWN
19: LUCKY NUMBER: LENE LOVICH
20: QUESTIONS AND ANSWERS: SHAM 69
21: WAITING FOR AN ALIBI: THIN LIZZY
22: I DON'T WANNA LOSE YOU: KANDIDATER
23: JUST WHAT I NEEDED: THE CARS
24: THE LOGICAL SONG: SUPERTRAMP
25: GOODNIGHT TONIGHT: WINGS
26: FOREVER IN BLUE JEANS: NEIL DIAMOND
27: REMEMBER THEN: SHOWADDYWADDY
28: POP MUZIK: ROBIN SCOTT

29: VALLEY OF THE DOLLS: GENERATION X
30: THE STAIRCASE: SIOUXSIE AND THE BANSHEES
31: KNOCK ON WOOD: AMII STEWART
32: HAVEN'T STOPPED DANCING YET: GONZALEZ
33: CAN YOU FEEL THE FORCE? REAL THING
34: FIRE: THE POINTER SISTERS
35: HALLELUJAH: MILK AND HONEY
36: INTO THE VALLEY: SKIDS
37: THE MEMBERS: OFFSHORE BANKING BUSINESS
38: KEEP ON DANCING: GARY'S GANG
39: IMAGINATION: ROCKY SHARPE AND THE REPLAYS
40: LET'S FLY AWAY: VOYAGE

TOP TWENTY GROSSING MOVIES IN THE UK: 1979

1: Moonraker
2: The Bitch
3: Alien
4: Life of Brian
5: Rocky II
6: Every Which Way But Loose
7: Star Trek: The Motion Picture
8: The Black Hole
9: Quadrophenia
10: 10
11: Halloween
12: The Deer Hunter
13: National Lampoons Animal House
14: Apocalypse Now
15: Superman
16: Scum
17: Porridge

18: Manhattan
19: Jaws 2
20: Yanks

SPORTSNIGHT

BBC ONE
 Wed 4th Apr 1979,
21:35 on BBC One
Introduced by Harry Carpenter
Action, news, personalities and opinion from home and overseas including tonight:
Cup Soccer Action
Highlights of a top match
Commentator JOHN MOTSON
The Man in the Corner
' I think of myself as a psychiatrist, father-confessor, mother-superior, and maid of all work.'
The words of Britain's most successful boxing manager, Terry Lawless.
After taking John H. Stracey to Mexico to win the world welterweight title, Lawless achieved a unique double last month when he took a second British fighter abroad to become World Champion-Maurice Hope. And later this month another champion from the Lawless stable, Scotsman Jim Watt , goes for a world title in Glasgow.
HARRY CARPENTER profiles the former shipping clerk whose talented squad of 12 boxers also includes champions Charlie Magri , Jimmy Batten and John L. Gardner.
Soccer television presentation ALEC WEEKS
Film director JOHN WATTS ProducerJOHN PHILIPS
Editor JONATHAN MARTIN

"It was a wonderful summer of dreams, followed by a winter of discontent, but even amongst such freezing rain, icy snow and bitter cold, I always had the reds." John Ludden

...79, when you had to sit by the transistor radio in your bedroom for the second half football commentaries. Sometimes, there was such frustration as the sound dipped in, out. You would have to shake, move it around until the game was back in your world. Scream at the tuner! That never worked. *BBC Radio 2*, and none better than the Welsh wordsmith Peter Jones to guide you through the pain, angst, torment and joy of a football match. As you built pictures on the canvas of your mind, Jones' rich voice crackled out and filled the air around you with a gold dust. It's hard to describe looking back now, but, magic occurred, on the radio...

INTRODUCTION:
OUR FRONT ROOM

In my mind's eye now I can still see nana Norah sat at our dining room table in the front room staring at the transistor radio, and me opposite doing the same. Neither of us spoke we just listened. Mum was also knocking around doing a bit of cleaning, never really getting this football business. She did tell me if United score not to go crazy? See what I mean about not getting it? Nana got it, she was a pure red, I think I got this madness off her more than anyone. She also got the dislike for Liverpool, but I think that came much further on from 79, as nana would always go on to refer to the Scousers as ''God's team'' for the way they appeared to get all the luck, not because he himself upstairs actually held a candle for them. Heaven forbid. So, here we were, me and nan, with mum on the bench. The noise of the crowd and the BBC Radio commentator filling our Rosslyn Road world with his dramatic words. There was thirteen minutes remaining at Goodison Park on the night of Wednesday 4th April 1979, (a school night), the FA Cup Semi Final Replay between our beloved Manchester United and Liverpool. 0-0, we had played so well they said, somewhere in the Goodison *Park End* was dad, I shut my eyes, I could see him. ''What happens if it's a draw?'' asked mum. ''Do they both go to Wembley.'' I glared across as she dusted down her Stylistics records, and daren't answer, I simply tutted in disgust. United had the ball, nan looked at the clock: ''Hope your dad (my grandad Bill) doesn't forget his key Maureen, he'll be off out now for the last hour in the Ben Brierley. He's like bloody clockwork!'' Suddenly, United had the ball...

"Bailey plays it straight into the Liverpool half...A challenge from Jordan...Breaks to Mickey Thomas...

That's for later!

ACT ONE:
"WEMBLEY! WEMBLEY! WE'RE THE FAMOUS..."

Wembley stadium.

It was Saturday 12th May 1979, a late, now very grim summer's afternoon. I never slept a wink last night. I got up at the crack of dawn; I'd been out and picked up the newspapers for the Cup Final pull-outs. Such bundles of sheer joy under my arm. The player interviews, who were the experts picking to win? Worryingly most were going for Arsenal, but what did they know I told myself, whilst waiting for BBC Cup Final Grandstand to start. Always BBC in our house. Nothing to do with tradition, just the ITV adverts were so annoying. I looked at the clock, four hours to kick off, three hours, forty minutes to *Abide with Me*. I checked once more the Cup Final programme Dad had bought me, (I still have it). It's front cover showing the trophy on a mound of grass with both United and Arsenal rosettes. The words **CUP FINAL** in large white letters, then followed by Arsenal v Manchester United beneath. Cup final day in its infancy, but that was then. This, sadly now for with Just four minutes remaining of the Final, the Gunners were 2-0 up and coasting. My day of dreams had slowly evolved into deep, bitter disappointment. First half Arsenal goals from Brian Talbot and Frank Stapleton had sunk United, who though fighting for every ball lacked any spark or real imagination. On what had been a stiflingly, roasting Wembley afternoon, here in Moston, similar, even though Dad had shut the curtains, what was once the perfect setting with plates of sandwiches and crisp now resembled a funeral wake. Call this the tiresome, deflated ramblings of a broken twelve-year-old, and you'd be completely correct. I felt sorry for all the United fans in the stadium, those red Mancunian hordes bedecked out in scarves and hats still singing loud and proud. Our banners all works of art such as **JORDAN PLANTS RICE!...**

Many there must've found their thoughts turning to just getting home for last orders. Drowning sorrows, simply drinking the gloom away. Then, oh, my God, goal! The reds pulled one back. From a Steve Coppell free kick a desperately tired looking Gordon McQueen, with socks down by his ankles just stretched out one of his long legs to poke the ball past Pat Jennings! Dad was off the sofa with his mate Billy Fitz. Home from Saudi Arabia, Billy was chief electrician at Saudi Airport and loved a drink. Those months of being stuck in that desert (no alcohol allowed), oasis, now behind him, as he was in the midst of drinking Moston dry. "They couldn't, could they, Johnny?" he asked my Dad. Who didn't reply, his eyes glued to the screen whilst filling up a beer glass without spilling a drop. Pure unadulterated genius. The noise from the United Wembley end suddenly increased from hopeful slumber to Concord level decibels, but big Gordon's goal was surely only a mere souvenir. What else could such a beautiful, but utterly useless thing be for? Back on the pitch United won the ball from the restart, Coppell's interception and pass forward found Sammy McIlroy. I was dreaming, this was cruel, it wasn't really happening. Onwards went Sammy, Dad and Billy were off the sofa, the last Busby Babe was in the penalty area, skipping past tackles like a child dancing through Mancunian raindrops. As we and the rest of the footballing world held a collective breath our other Belfast boy rolled a shot mere inches past Pat Jennings hands, and into the bottom corner! Utter madness ensued! Me, Dad and Billy hugging, laughing, screaming and dancing, I wanted to cry but daren't, then I saw a tear in Billy's eye as he filled up his Baileys glass! From abject despair to sheer jubilation. Football eh, bloody, bloody, bleedin' football. I loved this team so much; it was my life and probably will be till I'm old and grey. (Today). There could be only seconds left, our substitute Brian Greenhoff was getting ready for extra time another thirty minutes. I wasn't sure if I could handle it. The adults were okay, they had alcohol, what did I have? Dandelion and bloody Burdock.

Wait, where was Liam brady going? "Bring him down!" shouted dad
as Brady tore into our half being chased by a desperate tiny duo
of Lou Macari and Mickey Thomas-he played it wide left to Graham
Rix, whose lofted cross sailed over a stranded, hapless Gary Bailey
who'd come too far, the ball landed at the feet of Arsenals striker
Alan Sunderland, with just an open goal to aim at.
But I'm going to stop it here, because, let's be honest,
Manchester United had already won their real Final in the FA Cup
that year. This book is dedicated to an early April Spring evening on
Merseyside at Goodson Park. How as just a young kid my love for
United was signed, cemented and sealed listening to the match on the
radio with people I loved.
This is the story of 79.

ACT TWO:
FOOTBALL, SCHOOL AND MORE FOOTBALL!

We lived in Rosslyn Road,
just off Moston Lane in North Manchester. It was a red house, a
Labour house. Irish and Collyhurst descent. It was a Manchester
United house. On the night of the game my dad (Johnny)was at
Goodison. He was a spark working in Carrington at the time and
travelled to Merseyside in a car with his mate Pete Cassidy. Me, I'd
spent the day as a first year at Saint Matthew's Roman Catholic High
School planning tactics for our manager Dave Sexton, so he didn't
have to bother. That Wednesday my mind was far away from double
English, RE and woodwork with a mad Ukrainian teacher, whose
name I could never pronounce and now can't even remember. My
greatest achievement in there, I carved out a horse that looked like a
hedgehog, and my mum (Maureen, mostly Mo), had it pride of place
on the front room cabinet for years. Beauty is in the eye of the
beholder they say. The hedgehog with a hump is still there, though
now it's lost pride of place to framed photographs of wide-grinning
grandchildren. Come school dinner time I'd be sat on the grass verge
at the edge of the playing yard. Behind me over the fields, the huge
Moston Mill with a tall poking chimney behind it. Around my ears,
the chatter of youthful, excited voices, the screaming, the laughing, I
was oblivious to all. There was serious work to do with my pen and
small notebook that had "MUFC OK" scrawled on the front. I'd step
through a magical door, a little like Mr. Benn entering a new world,
and try to figure out how the bloody hell United were going to beat
that lot. We'd matched them at Maine Road the previous Saturday,
2-2, now to reach the FA Cup Final, we had to play them again.
Those down the East Lancs Road, Liverpool. In Star Wars terms,
though no great fan they were the Death Star to me. A little bit of
Liverpool's dark mystique had recently been shredded by having their

European Cup, and League champion's status stripped off them by Brian Clough's, brilliant, Nottingham Forest's, rebel alliance. God bless them. This apart they remained in my life the big, bad Scouse wolf. Them and Maths. I also had some mates at home of blue Manchester City persuasion. Annoyingly close ones as well, once upon a time. There were occasions especially come Derby day when friendship was put away with the altar boy cassocks and Raleigh bikes and you simply kept out of each other other's way. Still do. David Hill, (Hilly) and Ian Ashley, (Ashy), Moston lane dwellers opposite the famed Golden Apple Fish and Chip shop. God, those Friday night queues for that place. I was sent after school as we only lived nearby. This chippy had legendary North Manchester status, indeed I even had an uncle who travelled from foreign climes, (Heywood) just to buy the gravy. Life, though for this Moston kid, when I wasn't queuing was all about football.

ACT THREE:
"ARGENTINA!"

My footballing awakening took place leading up to the summer of 1978. Manchester United was becoming an increasing presence in my life. Memories of the 1976 and 1977 FA Cup finals are vague. I didn't care enough to cry back then when Southampton's Bobby Stokes fired home his offside goal past Alex Stepney, but I felt the deep disappointment in our house. As indeed the elation twelve months on, when United ended Liverpool's treble dream and Tommy Doc danced and danced round Wembley with the cup in front of an adoring red army. No, for me football truly took hold shortly afterwards. The 1978 World Cup to use a Catholic metaphor as I'm of that particular tribe, Saint Dunstan's church sitting grandly on Moston Lane was my true baptism. Memories beforehand was being at my nana Norah's and grandad Bill's house at 21 Penn Street, and Bill tuning into BBC Wales, so we could watch the Welsh take on Scotland in the now legendary winner takes all match at Anfield. After bending, twisting, swearing and screaming at the aerial, he finally picked up a blurry, fuzzy picture, and I could just about make out our very own Martin Buchan crossing beautifully for Kenny Dalglish to score with a glorious header. I was hooked! Two wonderful teams with beautiful kits but it was the Scots who were off to Argentina and I with my World Cup wall chart would be watching with enchanted eyes.
My first FA Cup Final experience came also with grandad in the early summer, as we watched in North Wales at the family caravan near Towyn. Ipswich beat Arsenal with a late Roger Osborne goal. I can still hear the great BBC commentator David Coleman almost bursting out of our small portable television, which shook like an earthquake every time a train passed on the railway line next to us under the sea wall. "Osborne! One nil!"

Earlier that Christmas,
 Santa Claus very kindly delivered me a Scotland kit in an Umbro
tube, which was left lovingly in the midst of a new Subbuteo
pitch with a Scottish team already lined up against Brazil. Not
forgetting the mighty grandstand with four supporters, a policeman, a
newspaper reporter, a television tower and two World Cup balls. I
also got the Manchester United tracksuit, truly a gift off the
footballing gods, never mind Santa. It didn't take much back then to
make a young kid think the world really was a most wonderful place.
Come the start of Argentina 78, I was in the last year of Saint
Dunstan's Juniors. The big school up the lane with uniforms and stuff
was coming into sight but not just yet, thank goodness. As for my
adopted bonnie Scotland, I sat there with dad watching open mouthed,
as they were ripped apart by the might Peruvians. Teofilo Cubillas,
Hector Chumpitaz, Juan Munante. Magnificent, foreign-sounding,
footballing names with the red stripe across their shirt making them
appear even more from another world. Teofilo, he of the bewildering,
swerving free kicks leaving Alan Rough standing haplessly still like a
traffic cone caught in a car headlights. A 3-1 beating and much worse
followed with a 1-1 draw against lowly Iran. Iran? They had kidded
me this lot, a lovely kit but that was about it. When one of my
favourite Manchester United players Martin Buchan-he was like
Fonzie off Happy Days but far cooler. A guitar playing Buchan
smashed his head open by running into fellow Scottish defender
Willie Donachie against the Iranians. A Manchester City player, I
suspected foul play. Maybe it was best if Scotland just went home
early with my other United players, Joe Jordan and Lou Macari in one
piece. To still qualify out of their group Ally MacLeod's fed up army
needed to beat the beautiful orange shirted Dutch by three goals. I had
done my homework on Holland. Even without their best player
Johann Cruyff, who I was so looking forward to watching, Johann had
stayed at home for fear of being kidnapped. What the hell that had to
do with football I had no idea back then. My shoot magazine which
was now dropping through our door every Thursday morning had

articles that spoke in glowing terms about him. Yet, the Dutch still had some fantastic world stars who all looked like they belonged on Top of the Pops. Johnny Rep, Arie Haan, Robbie Rensenbrink, the Van Der Kerkhof brothers, Willie and Rene, and their hugely impressive Captain Ruud Krol. This was a team of Panini football sticker giants. Elsewhere in the tournament host nation Argentina was set to be my new adopted team. It was a close choice between them and Peru. I ultimately chose the Argies because of their supporters and the spectacular confetti celebrations that covered entire stadiums whenever they played.

And a certain centre-forward called Mario Kempes.

What a footballer, long flowing locks, tall, with dancing feet, always looking to play one two's with his partner in crime, the moustachioed Mexican bandit look-alike, Leopoldo Luque. Appearing like he'd jumped right off the Magnificent Seven film set. As for the loyalty to the Scots, it was clearly a one-way thing. God only knows what Holland would do to them. I'd watched on television before the tournament began, when a journalist asked Ally Macleod what he was going to do after winning the World Cup. He replied: 'Retain it!''

I believed him, me and it felt like the whole of Scotland. After they couldn't even beat Iran, Ally was sat at a press conference with no friends left amongst the gathered hacks. He bent down to pat a stray dog at his feet, smiled, looked up and said: ''At least he still loved me.'' Then it bit him!

Astonishingly, Scotland finally turned up for the party and as I watched with dad, me in my Scotland top, he enjoying his Woodpecker cider, Archie Gemmill took off on amazing dribble through the Dutch defenders making it 3-1! Suddenly, they needed just one more goal to achieve a small miracle and qualify! I was off the sofa punching the air! My loyalty to bonnie Scotland now fully returned! ''They're going to do it dad, my boys are going to do...''

Then reality hit me in the face like one of those ice-cold snowballs thrown by one of those big lads from the North Manchester school, who ambushed me months before as I headed home. Johnny Rep had picked the ball up thirty yards out and as they held on tight to their beer pints in the pubs and bars of Glasgow and all points North of Hadrian's wall, as Rod Stewart started to pen a tribute song, Rep finally ended Ally's dream with an absolute screamer that Rough could only wave at. It was all over. Moston's biggest Scotland's fan became resigned to the inevitable and as United's former manager Tommy Docherty famously told the world: "We were home before the postcards," it was time to throw my lot in with someone else, and like nearly every other young lad in my year, I went with Argentina. It all came down for the home side to reach the final they had to beat Peru by four goals. This game would not kick off until around midnight here and it being a school week, and the fact no way could I stay awake, I drifted off, dreaming, praying Argentina would do it. Then, the sound of someone coming up the stairs into my bedroom and dad waking me up. "They've done it J!" he said, 'Argentina have won 6-0! They're in the World cup final!" There they would play the extended version of the Bay City Rollers. Holland. That Argentina beat the Dutch 3-1 after extra time caused scenes of unadulterated celebrations, not just in Buenos Aires but also in Saint Dunstan's playground as the chants of "ARGENTINA!" thundered loud from eleven-year-old voices! Those supporting Holland demanded a rematch but with thirty odd Mario Kempes' against five or six overwhelmed poor souls, the World Cup was easily claimed again. This time by a much larger score! Years later, I would write a book about the biggest fix in the history of sport, but such thoughts were not for that long gone Monday morning back in 1978, as "ARGENTINA" echoed loud outside the school fence, drifting towards Moston Lane.

And home.

ACT FOUR:
RELIGION, THE FOOTY'S BACK AND THE "WANDERIN' STAR"

My footballing fix for the summer was over, now was all about preparing for the real thing.
Manchester United.
As I waited for the First Division fixtures to be announced the awful dawning hit me that the six weeks holiday was over, the big school dawned. Saint Matthews RC High school. I hated school, I'm glad I still don't have to go. That first morning in the big schoolyard was horrible. Former "cocks" of Junior schools were being put with remarkable stealth precision to the sword. Soon as one was pointed out the older lads went to work. Luckily, this had nothing to do with me and I was bypassed! There would be bullies over time but I learnt fast you had to stick up for yourself. I was placed in St Vincent's house. Personally, I'd never heard of him. Best years of your life, not likely, I just wanted to keep my head down and get it all over with. My first teacher there was a nice, but quietly menacingly Irish lady called Mrs Murden. She turned out to be my favourite teacher in the hated four years I spent there. In our first lesson we had to stand up and give our full names. I remember one lad called Duncan Edward Scott. Close I thought, but just not good enough.
Like dad and grandad Bill said there was only ever one Duncan. Slowly the eternal summers of those years you thought would last forever ended and the football season came back into sight. The fixture list was studied until I knew it by heart. City at home on 30th September, Liverpool at home on Boxing Day, please Santa, please! City away on 10th February, the day before my birthday, don't you dare let them ruin it reds and finally, 14th April, Liverpool away. The four that truly mattered. Before the opening league match at home to Birmingham city on 19th August, we had another game at Old

Trafford. A friendly against the great Real Madrid to celebrate our centenary of being formed in nearby Newton Heath 1878. Home also one time to my other (Irish) nana and grandad's pub, Norah and Jack. The Cloggers Arms. It stood at 288 Oldham Road, set off from the canal next to the local Co-op store which sold some great toy soldiers, and was well known known locally for its grand clock tower. They also had the Old Loom, a true "Irish pub" on Moston Lane. I loved it there. The pub is still standing today but shut down. I developed a little money making scam in my much earlier showbusiness career years. I was about seven-years-old and in the Old Loom vault where there just happened to be a piano. Once the Guinness was kicking in with the Irish punters to top up the previous night's bevvy, and with one of the more sober clientele on the piano, I'd serenade them with Lee Marvin's "Wanderin' Star" from the musical Paint Your wagon. Once finished and the tumultuous applause had died down I would go around with a hat to collect my wages. The regulars were generous to a fault, mainly I think to ensure I only sang once. Nana Norah was rightly treated like a Queen in that place. There was great trust between her and the men of the vault. So much that when it came to after hours, nana would leave the keys, go to bed and let them serve themselves. Come the next morning the takings would be waiting for her correct to the last penny and the vault spotless.

Back to the reds,
 early signs were more than promising for Sexton's soldiers as they thrashed Real Madrid 4-0. Sammy McIlroy and Jimmy Greenhoff with two apiece. Before the game began there was a parade of Supporter's Club branches and a host of United's Post-War stars were presented to the 49,397 crowd. Last onto the pitch to an emotional deafening reception finally appeared a smiling Sir Matt Busby and Jimmy Murphy, the pair who led us back from the tragedy of Munich. In 1978, for me by far they were the greatest team the world had ever seen. I was though remember incredibly biased and just eleven. The Manchester United team that started the match…

Roche, B Greenhoff, Albiston, McIlroy, McQueen, Buchan (Captain), Coppell, J Greenhoff, Jordan, Macari and McCreery.
 Though it did end with a flurry of substitutions including Alex Stepney in his last season who even saved a penalty. This was the first result that really mattered to enter my notebook and it read lovely. Manchester United 4 Real Madrid 0.

The opening day of any football season always has the sun shining bright, casting late afternoon shadows, newspapers pull outs and your hopes sky high for the following nine months of Saturday heaven. Whilst it felt like Christmas for Eve for me, the jury was still well and truly out for my manager Dave Sexton. This was his second campaign and the selling of The Stretford End crowd favourite and top scorer at the time, Gordon ''Merlin' Hill'' in April 78, to Derby County and Tommy Docherty, had left them raging. Sexton appeared a nice man, humble, a quiet man, too bloody quiet, claimed his many critics, but, how on earth do you follow the Doc? His interviews with journalists tormented them for they were used to a cascade of Docherty eye-catching quotes and behind the dressing room door tales. A nudge and a wink, you help me, I'll be good to you. The Doc's character was Machiavellian, a true character in all senses of the word. In comparison having to deal with the much more straight-batting, mundane Sexton must've been like pulling your own teeth out. Which reminds me of Chefs Dentistry on Moston Lane. The cries of terror from kids being dragged there by fed up mums often echoed loud to nearby shoppers. Chef was a man who made the child catcher from Chitty, Chitty, Bang, Bang appear like Jeffrey off Rainbow. Once, he scared the life out of my friend's sister. Taking revenge, armed with eggs we returned to his torture chamber later that evening and from the safety of the backstreet entry launched our eggs. Unfortunately, in the darkness we targeted the wrong building splattering the newsagent next door who lived above his shop, and who was a Salford Harrier long distance runner. He chased us for what seemed forever and I'm convinced that man is still running today. Not my finest hour.

Whilst Docherty's flamboyant entry into a crowded room could well have been serenaded by trumpets and dancing bears, equally Sexton's similar appearance would more likely have been hailed by a lone, weary piano man playing Simon and Garfunkel's "The Sound of Silence." A crowd used to Tommy Docherty's blistering, all-out attacking football. Two wingers, a midfield buzzing, electrifying pace and bewildering movement with orders fired from the bench to go forward be it home or away. Then there was Dave Sexton. In just a short period with mostly the same players United had been transformed into a far more functional team. Forwards were expected to chase back, something wholly alien to Gordon Hill, hence one of the main reasons he was let go. A public slap off Martin Buchan on the pitch helping him on his way. Sexton's style of football fitted his personality like a glove. The previous season's finish of tenth position hardly helped matters. His United had to do better, if you were going to play in a style that the punters hated some success was desperately required. A trophy. Although this only guaranteed a little more time. In just the nine years since Sir Matt stepped down the United hot seat resembled Joe 90's. Wilf McGuiness, Frank O'Farrell and Tommy Docherty, though to be fair the latter for far differing reasons, but the Doc I'm sure could still vouch that the job came with a crown of thorns. Tommy Doc will tell you he was sacked for "Falling in Love" with the wife of club Physio Laurie Brown. The rights and wrongs of what occurred. A sense existed of "He who wasn't playing away in the United hierarchy cast the first stone?" Docherty was clearly irked, he wasn't the only one, double standards clearly at work. A scenario debated endlessly, but the fact that Tommy was with Mary while in his nineties till passing tells you everything.
 You simply can't help falling in love.
  Maybe etching for a quieter life Busby went for Dave Sexton. Sad for the Doc because it was clear to all that after the historic victory over Liverpool in the 1977 Cup Final, Manchester United, Red Army and all were on the march both on the pitch and off it. A footballing giant on the verge of being awaken once more, but the man chosen to

Now carry the torch forward had neither the personality nor bravery to fully open its eyes.

The opening match.
 A programme costing fifteen pence and on its front cover a picture of the various United supporter's clubs on the pitch during the recent Real Madrid Match. So it began. On Saturday 19th August 1978, in front of 56,139, Manchester United opened their centenary season with a gruelling 1-0 win against Birmingham City, thanks to a Joe Jordan winner twenty minutes from time. At a stifling, nervous Old Trafford, big Joe's goal was greeted with more relief than joy. Nothing appeared to have changed from the previous season. Turgid stuff. Still, at this time I wasn't allowed to go on my own, that came a year later to be followed by a League Match book ticket throughout the eighties. Back in 78, I had a Saturday evening routine where firstly United's result was written with great care into my MUFC OK notebook. Elsewhere, for I was eager to drink in everything else that had occurred, the dreaded Liverpool had won 2-1 at home to QPR, whereas City drew 1-1 away at Derby. Then, come Five o'clock and the thumping, rousing music to accompany the BBC Radio Two's legendary Sports Report. A weekly sporting occurrence since Saturday 3rd January 1945.
Dee-dum, dee-dum, dee-dum, dee-dum, dee-diddely-dum, dee-daaah! I'd listen whilst gazing out through my bedroom window at the last days of this Moston summer. Across our road at the back of a croft, (more of that later), stood the tall spire of Saint Dunstan's church, looming large in case I dared to err and not tell all in the confessional box. I was eleven for god's sake, what was I going to do machine gun Bertaloni's ice cream van that visited our road? Religion has always fascinated and sickened me with equal passion. I'm no great fan to be brutally honest. It disgusts me today thinking back how teachers even in our Primary School found it okay to brutalise children. Whether it be garden canes, chalk brushes, strap belts or one particular character, a music teacher would you believe who got off by hauling kids off their seats, boys and girl by sideburns. Something when we reached

the last year he stopped doing, no doubt for fear of getting his face kicked in, rightly so. Like the Monkees I am a believer of sorts, far too many Our Father's and Hail Mary's down the line to claim not to be. I just don't trust those down here on Earth who claim to speak on his behalf. John Lennon had more than a point for me, I still have a word every night and talking about religion, once Sports Report had finished the football section, it was time to go and fetch Dad's Football Pink.

ACT FIVE:
KICK OFF, SUBBUTEO AND THE FOOTBALL PINK

After surviving five horrible long and turgid schooldays, the weekend could only truly begin at six thirty, when our local news programme Granada Reports finished, goodbye to Bob Greaves with the bionic glasses and Tony Wilson, (legend), flying off on a kite, or some other crazy adventure, maybe even introducing some band called Joy Division, and welcome to Kick off!

That season it became addictive. The whirling music-cut to the smiling, cheesy grins of Elton Welsby and Gerald Sinstadt to talk about the coming footy. Interviews with the managers and players. Who was fit or injured? Clips of previous matches. Goals, goals and goals! A small fix, but just enough to keep me going until the following day. Thirty minutes of pure joy even if I had to sit through the Manchester City and Liverpool sections. City wasn't so bad because they were up and down like us, but the Scousers? Ominous. They weren't just beating teams Paisley's men appeared on a mission to thrash everyone out of sight. Our turn would come Boxing Day, but, normally against the scousers United always appeared to up their game. Anyway, there was far more urgent, pressing matters to contend with before that lot rocked up in Manchester, for my Subbuteo World Cup tournament was well underway and with me being all sixteen teams, there was some serious flicking to do. All the games took place on a five aside Subbuteo pitch that I'd picked up on the Isle of Man. It was the perfect size for my bedroom floor and easy to play with five outfield players and a goalkeeper. The Isle of Man holds differing memories, wonderful and truly awful. I'd go on holiday there with my Irish nana Norah, whose friend owned a boarding house on the Douglas sea front, and we just so happened to be there when the Summerland complex fire occurred, killing fifty-one people in truly horrible circumstances. Memories are vague now, looking out the boarding house window and spotting the smoke drifting out the top of the building against a cliff drop. Also, I recall stood with my nan on the sea front watching later on as the fires blazed out of control-the terrible heat and a lady running past us, her face covered in blood. I do remember thinking she had no nose?...

Subbuteo, I'd mastered in my head the art of playing both sides at the same time. I even picked squads. Somehow, and it was never fixed, the teams played to how they did in real life. Italy, defensive, catenaccio, Scotland, terrible, Brazil, all flair, same with Argentina, the Germans? Well, they just won. As for England, we reached the final once but lost deservedly 2-0 to Bulgaria. For some reason the Bulgars were the exception to my theory and no matter how badly I flicked they always came good.

Back to reality,

   Gill Woods' Newspaper shop stood on the corner of Fold Street and Moston Lane. For the rest of the week it was a place that meant absolutely nothing to me, except woe-betide they ever forgot to deliver my Shoot magazine on a Thursday. I did have a friend who was very light fingered when it came to sweets and chocolates, and Gill prided himself on, ''Catching the little bastards!'' as he called the schoolkid Fagins. One time I was in there with my same light fingered friend, whilst Gill was boasting to a customer: ''These kids never get past me, eyes in the back of my bloody head, I have!'' Sadly, for Gill, they mustn't have been working that day for as I paid up for a lone Mars bar, once outside, my same, said friend shown me the vast fruits of his wizardry pilfering. Half a dozen chocolate bars, a packet of salt and vinegar Golden Wonder crisp, (only the best), spangles, love hearts, a handful of black jacks and even a double lemon dip which he hoisted especially for my mum. I always liked that. Anyway, back to Saturday evening, around ten to six I'd set off the short distance to Woods and on reaching Moston Lane find the same familiar faces already in place outside the shop across the road. I'd enter and it would be packed inside, all exchanging small talk with the main man Gill. A few would be clutching programmes having just come back from the match. Either by car or the 112 bus from the Ben Brierley stop that dropped you off at the top of Warwick Road.

"How was it?" someone would ask them, as I listened on intently. "Fuckin' shite mate," came the reply. "Sexton's football is dull as fuck," said another. I nodded sage-like, not that anybody saw me, or indeed cared. The chit chat continued until just after the clock struck six there was a sound of screeching tyres as a small van came to a sudden halt outside. The pink had arrived! In a slick operation of Mostonian perfection the package containing the newspapers was picked up, passed inside by another, for Gill to untie the banding strings with scissors on the counter, and in we went. Having already paid, you was in and out like the SAS. Whilst reading the headline many times I was nearly run over on the Lane being so deeply engrossed. It was a beautiful thing to hold, the smell of it, it smelt of football. So many riches insides. Hello old friend, it's been a long summer.

Welcome back!

ACT SIX:
CHEERS JOCK

An early War of the Roses midweek game loomed large for four days on from the opening day win over Birmingham City, my reds were away to Leeds, Leeds, dirty Leeds United. Following gentleman Jimmy Armfield being shafted for want of a bigger name by the Leeds board, former Celtic managerial great Jock Stein was brought in. Treated with utter contempt by his own board after stepping down from the manager's job, Stein refused their offer of looking after the Celtic Pools. Their Pools? This the same man who delivered the European cup to Celtic eleven years previous to become the first British club to win it a year before my own. After such a monumental achievement Stein should've been given the keys to Parkhead, instead they offered him the Pools? Thus, when Leeds chairman Manny Cussins came calling, big Jock took him up on his offer, but the two never actually shook hands. Come the Wednesday, Stein had yet to sign a contract and Jimmy Armfield's, Don Revie's and the short lived Brian Clough's assistant Maurice Lindsay, remained in charge of picking the side, after doing so in an opening 2-2 draw at Arsenal. Sexton went with an unchanged eleven from Saturday and a special West Yorkshire welcome was guaranteed for two former Leeds players Joe Jordan and Gordon McQueen. Twenty two years before Eric Cantona told his adoring followers that he didn't know why he loved them, he just did then signed for Manchester, the proper United, a transfer proving the catalyst for a first league title heading to Old Trafford since 1967, Jordan and McQueen also tread that same path. The first steps in Sexton dismantling Tommy Doc's team and building one in his own image, God forbid. Though to be fair both players swiftly became huge favourites on the Old Trafford terraces. First to jump ship and see sense was Jordan the previous January for £350,000. To be followed by the sound of double, righteous Yorkshire indignation a month later by fellow Scottish international McQueen, who came for £500,000. The tall, leggy defender with the scraggly mass of blond hair didn't help matters when in his own, sardonic manner on the deal being concluded, wonderfully declared: "Ninety nine per cent of players want to sign for Manchester United. The others are just liars."

This just after a fortnight earlier in my beloved Shoot magazine that he was quoted as saying: "I want to stay with Leeds United for the rest of my career!" You could hear the gnawing of teeth and the howling across the Pennines from our back garden. The actual match as I listened on *Piccadilly Radio 261* was traumatic enough. The coverage itself, report snippets and goal flashes in the middle of songs was enough to severely trouble an eleven-year-old who was a nervous individual at the best of times! United finally edged it 3-2 in what could best be described as a bitterly, hard fought encounter with no prisoners taken both on and off the pitch. The red army crossed the mountainous Pennines unlike Hannibal with elephants, but by trains, Salford Van Hire and large fleet of various vehicles with red scarves and flags hanging out of the windows. Joe Jordan had already played against Leeds at Old Trafford in the second half of last season thus already had faced their fans "Judas!" chants, but as the Guardian wrote at the time: "McQueen got both barrels back at his old hunting ground. Mob queries about his parentage as well as his value as a player." Gordon was also not just serenaded on his return he found himself pelted with anything the Leeds fans could get their hands on. So, it felt only right McQueen opened the scoring with a fine header, before Leeds equalised through their fellow centre half Paul Hart, signed from Blackpool to replace him. A thrilling match ensued with the reds going back in front just before half-time. Jordan heading on to Sammy McIlroy making it 2-1. Oh, how Elland Road was enjoying the return of their adopted Highland clan. A Frankie Gray penalty levelled for Leeds in the second-half only for Lou Macari to grab a later winner after being set up by yet another Elland Road favourite. My beloved Jimmy Greenhoff.

What a Wednesday school night!

Two games in unbeaten and as the result was added into the MUFC OK notebook, the thought of that horror trek of cross country in Boggart Hole Clough the following day, for once left my mind. At least for a little while. "Keep it going reds," I said quietly to myself whilst scribbling down the result. Oh, and just to finish Jock Stein saw the light and never signed that Leeds contract, seemingly it had all been a ploy to gain more power off the SFA, before taking on the Scottish national job. Like Brian Clough, Stein was at Elland Road for just forty four days. To Leeds disbelief even though it was them who acted to remove Clough, lightning had struck twice. You had to laugh! I regarded this as Scottish payback for what had occurred during the summer. Honour had been restored, at least in my red eyes anyway. Cheers Jock.

(Elsewhere, Liverpool won 3-0 away at FA Cup winners Ipswich Town with goals from Souness and Dalglish, two).

ACT SEVEN:
TWELFTH

Twelfth…
For some reason every time we did house cross country in Saint Vincent, I came twelfth. Not too bad considering there was thirty odd and more competing. When I say competing there were some who clearly cheated. One in particular, no names but this kid smoked, drank and his asthma was worse than mine, yet he was still always over the finishing line when I finally staggered over. I never ever saw him or his accomplices. This particular one would've also had to have been on a fucking skateboard to beat me-yet he did so, every time? The running course itself was brutal, taking in the full length of the sprawling Clough. This included paths stretching high across rolling fields, through streams, down hills, up high and on, and…Now, I wasn't by no means unfit, I could hold my own. I held out no dreams of making the 1980 Moscow Olympics as some precocious Moston kid who ran like the wind. Absolutely nothing of the sort, I plodded simply onwards never looking back, or stopping, for quite simply I'd never start up again. There were those who cheated, it was well known a short cut existed around the back of the boating lake down through the trees and to a spot near the finishing line, but out of sight of the game's teachers. One time somebody slipped up and the cheats were literally caught red handed sneaking through the bushes ready to make their entry onto the race. All hell exploded! The headmaster was swiftly informed as severe punishment was required to save their wicked souls. This strange Catholic need for wrath against young kids. Reminiscing now cheats or not it was scandalous. Led back to school as if about to be crucified, handed an incoming treble thrash of a buckled belt strap down onto their hands. Jesus wept…Me, that particular day? I came twelfth.

ACT EIGHT:
"BUZZER" AND THE BOYS

Saturday 26th August 1978.

They called him the smiling Pope, his Holiness Pope John Paul 1. My lot had a new boss. He came across on the television as a nice man with a warm smile. He promised change, to make things better, and as the Manchester sun continued to shine and the white smoke drifted high in the Rome sky, Manchester United travelled to Bobby Robson's FA Cup winner's Ipswich Town and got turned over horribly 3-0. Again, my soft spot for the other team taken advantage of. I'd supported Ipswich in winning the Cup against the Gunners and this is how they repaid an eleven-year-old? 3-0? All the fun I'd had watching that game with grandad at our caravan in Wales disappeared over a ninety-minute period of goal reports, courtesy of switching from Piccadilly 261, Radio Manchester and Radio 2. No loyalty in this game, I was learning fast. Paul Mariner right on half-time, then, two late strikes from Mariner again and Brian Talbot. The latter would move to Arsenal the following January for £450,000 and our paths would cross once more in early summer. Already there was bad rumblings at Gill Woods newsagent waiting for our Pinks, as both team's defeats were discussed and dissected. For that same day Liverpool played Manchester City at Maine Road, and thrashed them 4-1. Two goals from Graeme Souness, one each for Ray Kennedy and Kenny Dalglish. A rather ominous result for the rest of the season. General consensus amongst us lot, me obviously saying nothing just appearing equally frustrated as everyone else, was that the Scousers would be the team to beat once more. "They might be fucking, horrible bastards," said a thoroughly fed up looking blue, who had been to Maine Road to witness the massacre. "But they're fucking, horrible, brilliant bastards!" We all nodded in agreement. Watching the game on Match of the Day later that evening Graeme Souness and Kenny Dalglish looked devastating together for Liverpool. This result

would ease mickey taking on Monday morning in school, also around
the streets of Moston, for with both reds and blues fans being given a
hiding neither could hold their heads high. As for United, a swift
chance to recover from their East Anglican debacle would come in the
League Cup the following Wednesday against Fourth Division
Stockport County, who had switched the game to Old Trafford after
originally being drawn at Edgeley Park for financial reasons. Also,
the Stockport hierarchy had no desire to see the red army swarming
all over their ground with the distinct possibility of dismantling it, if
the mood took them. Stockport's player manager was someone well
known to Manchester football, a certain Mike "Buzzer" Summerbee.
A former City legend, but to United fans hardly Mr Popular and we
looked forward to handing Buzzer and his team a proper drubbing.
So, went the plan for come the night all hell kicked in.

With a healthy 41,631 crowd,
  no doubt delighting the Stockport chairman Freddie Pye, who had
arranged for the entire game to be filmed on a Super 8 camera from
the Director's box. "Evidence for the jury your honour!"
  What should have been nothing more than a very decent payday for
Stockport County came so close on the pitch to being something very
special. With Summerbee leading by example, the old skill and fire
still evident Stockport were by far the better side in a first-half where
United simply never played. Against the run of play a fantastic cross
by Irish youngster Ashley Grimes set up Joe Jordan's diving header to
put us in front on thirty-seven minutes, but this apart it was awful
stuff from the reds, and the crowd were letting the players know.
Come half-time, the mumblings of discontent drifted over the Old
Trafford crowd. Hopes that stirring words from Dave Sexton could
rouse his troops from their slumber proved false as Stockport
amazingly continued to dominate playing United off the park. Their
veteran, bulky centre forward Les Bradd and Summerbee himself,
both tested Paddy Roche before finally the visitors got a much
deserved equaliser from the penalty spot. After Roche was forced to
bundle down Stuart Lee, (Signed a year later by Malcom Allison for

Manchester City), defender Alan Thomson stepped up to confidently fire past Roche igniting joyous scenes behind that same goal from Stockport County's delirious blue and white travelling army! Game on-still Buzzer's lads kept going and as the home fans watched on with ever increasing fury and dismay at their own team's ineptitude, United's kamikaze-at times offside trap failed, and the darting twenty-one-year-old Scouser Terry Park brushed off Brian Greenhoff, to shoot past a diving Paddy Roche into the far corner. 1-2 and disaster loomed large for Sexton's soldiers. It had been no fluke with Stockport thoroughly deserving to be in front. The mood on the home terraces was hardly helped when on taking a corner a smirking Mike Summerbee wiped his hands on the flag. The old City dog was loving it! Finally, as the clock ticked down the famous Stretford End late charge roared loud, and Gordon McQueen, with just three minutes remaining acted in a manner that typified United's performance by getting himself sent off after flooring his former boot boy at Leeds, Derek Loadwick for sitting on the ball! Cue utter mayhem as Sexton's assistant Tommy Cavanagh attempted to drag big Gordon off the field before he did any more damage. Summerbee appeared on the scene to have his customary fiver's worth taunting the Scottish international. Words but nothing more were exchanged and referee Peter Willis, a former Police Officer from County Durham added time on and the game continued to its bitter/sweet finale. Despite tormented by their team's showing the Old Trafford crowd as if inspired by McQueen's crazy dismissal raised the decibel once more. Entering injury time, Stockport's keeper Mike Rogan ignored the deafening Mancunian whistles and boos in his ears as he attempted to take his time kicking the ball clear, only to be utterly shocked when Willis penalised him for appearing to overstep the area, and handing the reds an indirect free kick on the edge of the box. A last chance for salvation as Grimes tapped aside for Sammy McIlroy to mishit, only for Rogan to let the ball bobble past and into the net. 2-2! Saved at the last. As the Stockport players led by Buzzer raged at Willis, a replay dawned once again here at Old Trafford and more cash in the pot for Chairman Freddie! The game entered its dying embers-Willis checked his watch

s United fullback Arthur Albiston lumped a long and hopeful high-ball into the Stockport County area where Rogan jumping with fellow defender Thompson and Joe Jordon appeared to win out-yet Willis pointed to the spot? A penalty for United, but for what? As white shirts gathered around him pleading, Willis laughingly claimed Thompson had hindered Jordan. It was a scandalous decision, but as Jimmy Greenhoff lashed a manic, undeserved winner then buried his hands in relief, Old Trafford embarrassingly erupted, and Mike Buzzer' Summerbee exploded at Peter Willis! The game finished 3-2, as for Willis, it was refereeing of the most bizarre kind. Manchester United had escaped over the wall of Strangeways Jail. Come the end, Summerbee led his players on a baiting lap of honour as he himself was given both barrels by reds, but his players warmly applauded for their grand efforts. "The glory and credit must go to them," said Sexton, post-match. "They really worried us." Only fair to leave the last word with a still raging Buzzer: "The game speaks for itself, that's all I have to say." Next in the League Cup for United would be third Division Watford, but I held no fear that my red shirted heroes would be fooled again. No chance.
Elsewhere, Liverpool lost 1-0 away to Second Division Sheffield United at Bramhall Lane to prove they were human after all).

ACT NINE:

SEPTEMBER DRAWS, THE CHAMP IS BACK AND SLEEP WELL, POPE JOHN PAUL 1

As the sun continued to blaze in the Manchester skies throughout a glorious September, four draws, all 1-1 followed in the league for Manchester United. Two home, two away. There was nothing shining or sunny about our football though, just dull. It was if a light had dimmed badly since the Docherty era came to its brutal end. Manchester United still played in sporadic moments some wonderful football, but I fear that was pure flashbacks, old habits dying hard. The Doc's spell that had been cast took some shaking off, but United were getting there for we were Dave Sextons team now. Firstly, at home in front of a 53,982 crowd with only a minute left to play, a thirty yard thunderbolt from Captain Martin Buchan earned a 1-1 draw. A typical United were on show with Everton leading from an early first-half Andy King strike, the reds meandering on seemingly resigned to defeat, only for a late rally inspired by the crowd, and cool Martin's magnificent strike saving the day. I always hoped he would write a song about that goal and play it on his guitar to the other players forever more!
(Elsewhere, Liverpool recovered from their shock midweek League Cup exit to massacre Tottenham Hotspur 7-0 at Anfield. Two each for Dalglish and Kennedy, plus three more from Johnson, Neal and McDermott. The later arguably one of the great goals of the seventies).

Next for Manchester United, away at Queens Park Rangers where a Jimmy Greenhoff goal saw a point earned, but it was yet another lacklustre display. Dave Sexton's former team now a shadow of what they were under him, but well deserving the 1-1 scoreline. The red army was becoming increasingly restless, they were angry with

Sexton. Blind loyalty could only be expected in troubling times if the football, as in Tommy Docherty's charge stirred your footballing soul, and encapsulated what United was all about, but when that style was compromised to a degree of being unrecognisable, then you were in deep trouble. Grumblings were becoming ever louder and if the vast ranks of the Streford End and their travelling clans turned, then Sexton and all his underperforming soldiers would feel the heat. (Elsewhere, Liverpool won 3-0 at Anfield against Birmingham City, with two goals from Souness, and one for Kennedy).

The previous February,
 I'd been so upset when Muhammad Ali lost his heavyweight title on points to Olympic champion Leon Spinks. At the finish he appeared broken, old. Ali's loss broke my heart, so as I woke early on Saturday 15th September 1978, and switched on the Tom Howard show on Radio 2, my heart jumped with joy. Their sports reporter Phil King was live from New Orleans at 7-30, our Moston time, informing that Ali had beaten Spinks in the rematch to win back his title at thirty two, and once more was champion of the world! I so loved Muhammad Ali, for he was bigger than life itself. The fight took place at the New Orleans Superdome in front of a record breaking 63,350 spectators, and a US television audience of ninety million. When the last bell rang and Ali's hand was raised high there wasn't a dry eye in the Superdome. This was the third time Muhammad had won the title back and despite calls for him to go out on top the great man would go on, and on, and tragically on...

That same day, 55,035 crammed into Old Trafford to see Manchester United take on the new League champions Brian Clough and Peter Taylor's, magnificent Nottingham Forest team. Last season Forest turned up and outclassed United 4-0 in a stunning performance. Many home supporters feared similar. The visitors remained unbeaten without really hitting any great form, but after beating Arsenal at home they had started to go through the old gears against United. It appeared another drubbing was on the cards when after just six minutes Ian Bowyer put the Champions ahead, however, United raised their game and finally drew level through Stevie Coppell on the half-hour. It was a thrilling encounter, the class of Forest clearly evident. Clough's men were halfway through knocking the holders Liverpool out of the European Cup and later claiming it as their own. We though despite a battling showing appeared light years away. (Elsewhere, Liverpool won 1-0 against Coventry, courtesy of a Souness goal).

Another Stevie Coppell goal saw the points earned a week on at Arsenal, but Sexton's United were kidding nobody, least their own fans and events were to get significantly worse. (Elsewhere, Liverpool fought out a 1-1 draw away with Ron Atkinson's exciting up and coming West Bromwich Albion side. Dalglish with their goal).

On Thursday 28th September 1978, grave news was broadcast worldwide from the Vatican, Rome, that Pope John Paul I (Albino Luciani), had died after just over a month. He was sixty-five-years-old. Being just eleven I was shocked at the gravitas of this news as it hit people I knew. Our family, my mate's mum's and dad's. The Catholic Dioceses of Saint Dunstan's went into mourning and come Sunday, mass was incredibly sombre. In years to come there was strange tales of murder, assassination, poison, but at the time it was just sheer shock for he appeared so much more human than past Popes. Genial and happy go lucky even. The headline in the Italian newspaper Corriere Della Sera, perhaps summed it all up best.
"His smile lasted only 33 days."
A beautiful epitaph.

ACT TEN:
DERBY DAY

We had our own football team,
the wonderfully named Crofton United. Based after the garage croft
we played on in the shadow of Saint Dunstan's church. Our best
quality was undoubtedly enthusiasm. Enthusiasm, oh, we had that in
bundles, but also some decent players. Two flying wingers in the form
of Hilly and Ashy, both city fans, Juniors Blues, Altar boys, they also
lived next door to each other. The best player by far though, cue a
drumroll, was easily Jackie who lived across from us on Rosslyn
Road. A girl! A bloody girl! An all-round player and probably my
best mate back then. Never to be messed with. A little like Bryan
Robson on the football pitch always standing out, not least for the fact
Jackie went to North Manchester High School for Girls, and it said a
lot for the rest of us that if there was ever any trouble we would line
up behind her. Our opponents were whoever fancied a game at the
time. Mostly local based but our Derby match was most definitely
Winnie Street: a collection of kids who lived mostly around there,
plus a few ringers. They were talented, very good. Others also risked
their hand against the might of Crofton, a certain team from near
Bogart Hole Clough who played not so much on a sloping pitch, but a
fully formed hill. This lot had mastered playing downhill to the extent
it was like the Brazil 70 team of Pele, Jairzinho and Carlos Alberto
coming for you at full pelt!. Also, if the ball was over-kicked it ended
up in what we called the hollows. The edge of the Clough which was
so very deep and for us mysterious. It was claimed to be by local
nutters and alcoholics the home of the legendary, ghastly little Bogart
creatures. These as a kid only ever existed in your head but that was
enough. Whoever put the ball down those steep foreboding hollows
had to go and fetch. I can still hear the groans now. When it came to a
playing kit we never bothered, except one time. Captain Jackie was
behind it and came up with a brand new club name. Goodbye Crofton

United, hello Blue Star! This was to be a Real Madrid all white kit, with an added blue star sewn onto the front of it by no guesses who? An idea was forming, this was always dangerous with us. To celebrate our rebirth we also bought a trophy from the Sports shop on Moston Lane. Hardly the Jules Rimet, but smart enough for our liking. For we were planning an inaugural match. It needed to be an opponent worthy of such an occasion, but couldn't think of anyone so approached Winnie Street. They swiftly agreed to a full size pitch, and even a referee-one of their dads. On a fine, Sunday afternoon, all roads led to Ashley Lane fields, (now a housing estate) and in front of a huge crowd by our standards, about six people, we got hammered 4-0. It was devastating to watch as they picked up the cup we had bought with our own money and ran back celebrating to Winnie Street. Bastards. It appeared the Blue Star kit was cursed and we ditched it the same day. That evening as we fumed about the defeat, it was decided Jackie would go around to the house of their Captain and retrieve our cup. Hopefully, Jackie's sweet-talking skills would be sufficient and she wouldn't have to hit him. How we cheered as she returned holding our cup a high!

We did buy it after all.

The real Manchester Derby was if possible, a much more serious affair, and it was taking place at Old Trafford on Saturday 30th September 1978. The butterflies in my stomach began soon as I woke up. Friendships were forgotten for a day or so, maybe even more if the result went really terrible. Since being taken apart by Liverpool 4-1 at home, Tony Book's City had slowly got their act together far more than United. They were lying in seventh place, three points ahead of us. Incidentally, their drubbing off the Scousers was put into some context when a revitalised Keith Burkinshaw's Tottenham Hotspur with their newly arrived, sparkling Argentine duo of Osvaldo Ardiles and Ricky Villa travelled to Anfield in great confidence, only to be massacred 7-0. The Scousers were not messing around.

The Derby.

Such a dangerous game that mattered so much. Those same butterflies grew increasingly worse as kick off drew ever closer. Interesting to compare the two sides.

THE TEAMS

Manchester United. Roche, Albiston, Houston, B Greenhoff, McQueen, Buchan, Coppell, J Greenhoff, Jordan, Macari and McIlroy.

Manchester City. Corrigan, Clements, Donachie, Power, Watson, Futcher, Channon, Owen, Kidd, (Yes, our Brian), Hartford and Barnes.

On paper there appeared little between them or indeed the managers, who both for me were like some of the boring teachers I was encountering at big school. One particular History teacher, a subject I actually liked had a way with him that I was convinced could turn off a light bulb from ten yards. There was one City player I had a sneaking respect for, but obviously I kept this quiet. It evolved from a Saint Dunstan school trip when we'd been taken to Maine Road. Peter Barnes signed my autograph book and we indulged in a short chat. The night previously he had played for England against Italy at Wembley, with himself on one wing, Steve Coppell on the other and we had won 2-0. I congratulated him on his superb performance, and Barnesy replied: "Cheers."
That was enough for me, blue or no blue. This was also the time of the Peter Barnes ball-the one with the string on that for a while whilst playing with it on your own you came to believe you were rather good! Its official title, The Peter Barnes Training Ball. Years later when Barnes joined United during the Ron Atkinson years, I loved watching him jinking and dribbling on the wing causing havoc, at least for a short while before a certain Scottish gentleman arrived from the far North of Scotland and dropped him like an anchor. Come

Three o'clock, I took myself off and my transistor radio to listen on our croft. My reason being that if we were turned over badly, I could possibly have been put up for adoption by mum and dad, due to the emotional breakdown that would duly occur as I smashed my bedroom to smithereens. No, I needed my eleven year old self space to deal with this. Therefore the croft it would be. Elsewhere, reds and blues if not at the game gathered around their radios in living rooms, bedrooms, bookies and pubs. The two blues most important to me would be sat in a parked up car shouting, ranting and raving about their lot being: "The boys in blue who never give in." Awful song. Hilly and Ashy had settled themselves in Ian's dad's car on Moston Lane. Me, here on the croft, well I was on safe ground unless we got beat then nowhere was safe. Same for them though, for if the reds triumphed I would hunt them down mercilessly. At least until six o'clock when I would have to go and fetch dad's Pink from Wood's newsagents.

I switched on the radio just in time for BBC Radio Two to announce at five minutes to three as was their tradition where the second-half commentary would come from. No surprise it was the Manchester Derby. I sat crouched down-the first half would be spent fiddling with the tuning knob into other channels to stay in touch. It sounded a scrappy game with neither team particularly impressive. United had most of the possession but no cutting edge, whilst City struggled equally also. The best player on the pitch by far as the game ensued was Steve Coppell who from the right was terrorising Scottish international full-back Willie Donachie. Ever so slowly as the second-half progressed the blues began to take charge. Gary Owen and Asa Hartford were digging in taking over the midfield. Chances were appearing for them and Brian Kidd, who owned a chippy near us, came so close to making the most of an error-stricken Paddy Roche fumble. Paddy worried me, the 55,000 crowd and it was clear he scared the hell out of Buchan and McQueen. Then, disaster, Mick Channon struck, oh god no! 1-0, my stomach churned-only for the goal to be disallowed for offside. My head pictured all this, my heart was thumping loud, I was never going to make twelve at this rate.

Time rolled on: the game appeared drifting to a scoreless draw, I suppose that was better than the horror of a home defeat. We were in the dying moments and United had a corner, I stared up at the back end of the enormous Saint Dunstan's church, remembering I still had a ball on one of their roofs. "Just give us one goal?" I asked. "Please!" Over came Coppell's corner to be met by a thumping McQueen header brilliantly parried away by Joe Corrigan. As the ball ran loose Joe Jordan pounced shooting low from nine-yards past a crowd of players into the net! Goal! We had scored! We had only gone and bloody scored! There I was jumping like a little madman on an empty croft thanking my Patron Saint! This football business was already turning me into a lunatic. I imagined inside the church the huge statue of Saint Dunstan winking and knowingly smiling: "My pleasure John lad!" The final whistle blew and as I punched the air, it was time now to go hunting blues, but first my MUFC OK notebook tradition. Out it came with pen also. This was a good one to add. Derby day eh?

(Elsewhere, a Jimmy Case hat trick handed Liverpool a 3-0 win at home).

ACT ELEVEN:
CANDLE IN THE WIND

Come the Monday morning,
and ingrained with memories of big Joe's winner against City, I
stepped back through the school gates ready to deal with whatever
crossed my path. I only had three days to wait until the reds were back
in action on the Wednesday, with Elton John's Third Division
Watford coming to Old Trafford in the League Cup. The Rocket Man
was arriving in town! No problem, I thought, we'd already suffered a
mighty scare against Buzzer and his Stockport County. This time
around Sexton would surely have the boys fired up. As for the big
school, Saint Matthews, though still early days I'd already come to
the dramatic conclusion that I hated it. Ninety five percent of the
people, (maybe a little generous) were fine, but no matter how hard I
tried to ignore the idiots always found a way into my face. Bullies
were something for me I learnt to deal with over a period of time. I
think there must have been some kind of unknown rule back then of
not being allowed to be quiet. It never happened too much but for me
once was enough. I took quite a bit until one day in the third year, a
Physics lesson, I hit back and from that moment the gobshites drifted
away. My one regret is not smacking someone on the nose in those
opening few weeks instead of kidding myself it was just normal,
because it isn't. To this day I despise bullies and it all goes back to
these supposed days of schoolyard dreams, wine gums and posers. I
had my reds, my own mates, my Subbuteo, I was a weird, a quiet, but
happy kid! There were others though I saw horribly brutalised by
these same people. Physically and mentally. Well, if they can live
with what I saw them do they're nothing like me.
Thank God.

Moving on to Wednesday 4th October 1978. What the hell has just
happened and who on earth is Luther bloody Blissett? I've sat

listening in utter disbelief as Elton John's yellow shirted Hornets have deservedly knocked out my team 2-1. It was no fluke, oh, Dave Sexton you're on very thin ground here. Where was your "Don't let it happen again!" speech? Do you realise what you've just done to me? No excuses as for Paddy bloody Roache? Where did we find him, the Mip Market? This man is not just giving out grey hairs to our poor defenders well before their time, I myself am ageing in dog years. A first-half in which we were almost totally overrun by their young, intelligent manager Graham Taylor's, dangerous, dynamic and ruthlessly direct team. Up front for them the thunderous power and pace of the young, Jamaican born Luther Blissett, and the tall gangly Ross Jenkins had us on cheese on toast for long periods. That United went in at the interval 1-0 up through Joe Jordan was akin to my mate robbing Woods' newsagents sweet counter. Daylight robbery. The lack of half-time words of wisdom from Sexton soon became apparent as the second-half restarted, and Roche came charging out of his penalty area like Batman on speed to deal with a rare misplaced, back-pass from Arthur Albiston. Paddy didn't just miss the ball, he had it taken off him by the hugely impressive Blissett. As Roche raced back into his goal the initial danger was cleared by McQueen, only for another cross to be launched from Watford's Bobby Downes. Throwing himself in the middle of Buchan and McQueen was Luther Blissett and his crashing header flew past Roche. 1-1, a stunning equaliser by Luther, a United fan himself. That night at Old Trafford a star was being born and he hadn't yet finished with us. Remarkably, Taylor had torn into his team at half time in the dressing room because he thought they weren't going for United's throats. Taylor was convinced we were there for the taking and as Watford continued to overrun us it came as no surprise on seventy-one minutes, that they took a deserved lead. Again, it was the brilliant Blissett who undone United by easily outjumping Albiston and Buchan at the far post to score with another header past a flailing Roche. So, it finished, boos rained down from the 40,534 crowd, and as the Watford players celebrated a famous victory, ours slumped off with shoulders down. Beaten and embarrassed. Hardly your archetypal club chairman, Elton

John couldn't hide his joy on being interviewed afterwards by BBC Sportsnight's Barry Davies, Elton spoke in glowing terms of Taylor and his side. Someone at Old Trafford obviously must've been a huge fan of his as "Candle in the Wind" was played over the ground tannoy as the great man held court.

A horrible epitaph of that evening was the racist abuse handed out to Luther Blissett during the game. Back then if not deemed normal, it was tolerated as nothing more than any of the other bile, abuse and vitriol hurled from the terraces. What made it even more sad when Luther was asked about it post-match, he all but shrugged it off as normal? "I'm a United fan, it's my first time here and I'll never forget it. The stick off the crowd never bothered me at all. People who resort to that are just ignorant, besides I've got used to this kind of treatment." A sad, tragic sign of those times. This vile racism would show itself again when a certain Three Degrees would come calling with gifts to Old Trafford shortly after Christmas. As for the reds, after being knocked out by Rocket man dark days loomed large. The Derby win now felt a long way off and for desperate Dave, he had better pull his finger out. Not a good one for the MUFC OK notebook but it went in anyway. I felt even back then that in this life you took the smooth with the bad. Oh, please, listen to me? Bloody hell! Eleven years old and United had already made me world weary. I'd be shaving next!

ACT TWELVE:
BREAKING CHAINS, AND POPE JOHN PAUL 11'S TOILET

Manchester United's form was like my schooldays, a couple of ups, but far more downs. We did return to winning ways the following Saturday with a hard fought 3-2 victory over lowly Middlesbrough, but it was far from satisfactory as the 45,403, Old Trafford crowd again struggled coming to terms with Dave Sexton's utter reluctance to let their players run free. It was football in chains with Sexton utterly refusing to bend. The Boro were struggling near the bottom of the table, but typically we made them look like a title chasing team, and it was no surprise when midfielder David Mills fired them ahead. This appeared to shock the reds into a reaction and come the interval we led 2-1 with a brace from Lou Macari. Sexton's half-time talk had its usual effect when Micky Burns equalised for Boro in the second- half, but ultimately the day was won when Joe Jordan pounced to grab a late winner.
(Elsewhere, Liverpool won 4-1 away at Norwich City. Two goals from Heighway, one apiece for Johnson and Case).

The next match away to Aston Villa and we're 2-0 down at half time, a John Gregory double after an insipid display. It was like being on a faulty rollercoaster with this lot. Dave Sexton must have stayed quiet at half-time because United roared back in the second half to grab a 2-2 draw. Five minutes after the break Sammy McIlroy pulled a goal back and then Lou Macari grabbed a deserved equaliser sending our away support wild! Come the final whistle United were unlucky not have won but this was truly a team struggling with its identity.
(Elsewhere, Liverpool won 5-0 at home. Two each for Dalglish and Kennedy, one for Johnson).

Rome. The Vatican.

Two days later on Monday 16th October 1978, there was a new head of the Catholic church. Fifty-eight-year-old Karol Józef Wojtyla, who was to be known as his Holiness Pope John Paul 11. The first non-Italian Pope in four centuries and now looking back widely regarded as one of the most popular. Born Poland, in a small town near Krakow, Pope John Paul 11 would come to Manchester in 1982, where 250,000 people, including me and a Saint Dunstan party walked all the way from Moston lane to Prestwich. How's that for true faith. Many years later I worked for a firm where one of the bosses was responsible for designing the Pope's own person toilet beneath the Heaton Park stage on which his Holiness would say Mass. He was also the first to test it and by all accounts it worked a treat. Happily, Pope John Paul 11's stay in the Vatican lasted a whole lot longer than his predecessor, (1978-2005), despite an attempted assassination in St. Peter's Square on Wednesday,13th May 1981. The Pope was shot and wounded by a Turk called Mehmet Ali Agca and despite being hit four times and suffering severe blood loss, he survived. The measure of the man shown itself when the Pope visited Agca in Jail, two years later and forgave him. Perhaps even more remarkable, in June 2000, at the request of Pope John Paul II, Mehmet Ali Ağca was pardoned and deported back home to Turkey.

Meanwhile, back in my little world the following Saturday at Old Trafford, matters went from bad to worse as Manchester United fell once more into a footballing abyss losing 3-1 to Bristol City. Again, it was no fluke as a Kevin Mabbutt's hat trick handed the away side two well deserved points. Their white shirts cutting United wide open at times. It was though a disastrous showing by the reds, defensively shocking-as for Paddy Roche, the error in letting go of the ball allowing Mabbutt to pounce for his third was nothing short of scandalous goalkeeping. It couldn't have been a coincidence that two renowned Scottish international centre halves had suddenly turned from outstanding solid defenders into Laurel and Hardy. On the terraces Roche was equally causing havoc for those with high blood

pressure and indeed them without it. The groans from all corners of the stadium as he fumbled for Mabbutt's final goal came laced with increasing disbelief and rising fury. It couldn't go on. Whilst Alex Stepney had fallen from Sexton's favour there was another, a young nineteen-year-old South African kid called Gary Bailey who was doing well in the Central League. Bailey had paid his own air fare to travel over for the chance of a trial at Manchester United and had done well enough to earn a contract. Tall, blond and commanding in his box went the reports. Whereas, currently our Paddy it was said had stopped giving autographs to the few remaining fans who wanted it in case he dropped the pen. My MUFC OK notebook was slowly turning into a horror story.
(Elsewhere, Liverpool won 2-0 at home to Chelsea with goals from Johnson and Dalglish).

Next, we were off to the Wolves and God only knew what United team would turn up at Molineux? Seven days on from the Bristol City debacle: wait for it. Wolverhampton Wanderers 2 Manchester United 4. Be still my red beating heart! After hitting the depths of despair against Bristol, (a little dramatic maybe), Sexton's soldiers rose and took apart an albeit struggling Wolves team stuck in the bottom three. It didn't begin so well for the reds when Gordon McQueen went off injured to be replaced by Ashley Grimes-with Brian Greenhoff switching effortlessly from midfield to centre half alongside the Fonz. Martin Buchan. Shortly after Brian's older brother Jimmy gave United the lead with a deflected effort that totally deceived the Wolves goalkeeper Gary Pierce who dived the wrong way. He added a second just seven minutes when after being put through by Joe Jordan's astute flick, Greenhoff slashed a wicked, left footed drive into the top corner that Pierce could only wave past him. Just when it felt the reds were finding a terrific rhythm step forward Paddy Roche somehow managing to let a low shot from Wolves Captain Kenny Hibbit, roll under his body into the net. Moment later he was at it again dropping the ball at the feet of striker Mel Eves, who somehow contrived to miss-but it was a close shave. Whatever thoughts going through the minds of United defenders having to deal with Roche's shocking mistake couldn't have been for my young ears. Right on half-time Brian Greenhoff stepped forward to slam a low shot past Pierce from the edge of the box and it was 3-1! Surely, not even a Dave Sexton team talk could stop us now? Matter improved even further eight minutes after the interval when from a magical Sammy McIlroy volleyed pass, Joe Jordan beat Wolves' offside trap to finish with great aplomb courtesy of a lofted chip into the far corner. 4-1, and big Joe found himself mobbed by red shirts. All was going swimmingly well for the big guy who only the day previous became the proud father of a first child, Lucy Jordan. Hopefully, he put his two front teeth back in when at home for Joe would have scared the poor kid to death. Still, the Wolves had a right go fighting for their first Division lives, Steve Daley smashed a fantastic twenty-yard shot past Roche to reduce the deficit, but it was nothing more. The game ended 4-2, a much needed tonic for both Manchester United players and fans. It was blatantly obvious to all that when Sexton let United off the leash we remained a threat to anyone home and away, but his natural tendency was to curb that adventurous streak, for it went against his footballing philosophy. It was though the United way and Sexton would've done well to embrace. We would be first on Match of the Day that night and I for one was set to enjoy while it lasted, because this team was absolutely capable of anything. Good and bad. (Elsewhere, Liverpool lost 1-0 away to Everton in the Merseyside Derby).

This point proved a week later when Manchester United started November by again stinking out Old Trafford with a 1-1 draw against lowly Southampton. United started promisingly where they left off against the Wolves when Jimmy Greenhoff struck early. Sadly, as the game rolled on the reds grew increasingly sloppy-error stricken, and it was no surprise when the Saints grabbed the equaliser in the second half from their midfielder Nick Holmes. The final whistle signalled yet another disappointing performance from Sexton's United. Bonfire night dawned but there were no fireworks at Old Trafford. We were flat. No rockets, roman candles, Catherine Wheels or even sparklers. The following night I watched on at a bonfire off Moston Lane when a dead black cat that had been knocked down was placed inside a tin biscuit box, and thrown into the flames.

 RIP Blackie.

(Elsewhere, Liverpool were held 1-1 at home to Leeds, their goal coming from a McDermott penalty).

ACT THIRTEEN:
THE SAINT ANDREW'S DAY MASSACRE

Firstly,

I'll just give you the date for I believed even at that stage of my writing career it was good to set the stage. Especially when it was nothing short of a footballing tragedy. At least in my young eyes. Saturday 11th November 1978. The venue in the Midlands. Saint Andrews Football ground. Our team, the guilty as charged that day. Roche, Nicholl, Houston, McCrerry, B Greenhoff, Buchan, Coppell, J Greenhoff, Macari, Jordan and McIlroy.

The final score, Birmingham City 5 Manchester United 1.

23,555 spectators were present including large numbers of the travelling red army who come the final whistle found even their legendary loyalty tested. Many already wearing Sexton out badges. Coming into the game Jim Smith's men lay bottom of the table with only three points and not a single win to their name, in fact they'd lost the last six. Their best player, the electrifying, young centre-forward Trevor Francis had been a terrible loss with a serious ankle injury, and had hardly played that season. So, it was the Blue's fans who turned up at Saint Andrews on that cold and bitter Birmingham afternoon, who must've feared the worse after what the reds had done to their fierce local rivals Wolves only a fortnight previously. Especially when in the early stages Lou Macari capitalised on some terrible defending, to set up Joe Jordan to fire past Birmingham goalkeeper Neil Freeman. 1-0 to United, it appeared the reds had turned up. Do I ever learn? Come half-time we were 3-1 down and it could have, should have been six. Irish international and former Manchester United player Don Givens caused havoc in the United defence who were badly missing the injured Gordon McQueen's aerial prowess. Big Gordon could jump so high he would knock pigeons out of the sky. It was Given's presence and perseverance that helped to set up

Kevin Dillon's twenty third minutes equaliser to fire past Paddy Roche, and ignite the Saint Andrews crowd! More home joy was to follow nine minutes later when their controversial Argentinian import entered proceedings. The mad and bad, crazy at times but simply brilliant defender Alberto Tarantini smashed a wickedly, curving free kick that caused mayhem and was duly finished off by Alan Buckley, with another assist from Givens. As United rocked, swayed and collapsed, Birmingham went for our throats. Another goal came right on half-time when the on-fire Givens robbed Brian Greenhoff to set up Buckley, who with an inch perfect chip over a stranded Paddy Roche's head made it 3-1! Incredible stuff from the bottom side and it got so much worse for the reds, when just after the interval Don Givens finished a magnificent move featuring Tony Towers, Mark Dennis, and Jimmy Calderwood, by slamming home a terrific header past a shell-shocked Roche, who was clearly working his notice, for he had been terrible once more. Much credence had to be given to Givens as he continued to lead the assault all afternoon on a besieged Manchester United penalty area. Whatever we tried failed to come off and to cap a most wonderful day for Birmingham City, and for him personally, Givens, helped by Tarantini set up Calderwood in the dying moments to make it 5-1. Total embarrassment for the Mancunians whose red faces were brighter than their shirts. As if the scoreline wasn't hard enough to take there was also a second-half incident between Brian Greenhoff and Alberto Tarantini, that ended with the United man being stretchered off after being knocked out unconscious by the fiery Argentinian. Missed by the referee and linesman, Tarantini quite simply got away with grievous assault. Mayhem ensued as an infuriated Joe Jordan who witnessed what occurred had to be dragged away from Greenhoff's assailant. Tommy Cavanagh also another was restrained. The World Cup winner Tarantini was bought for £295,000 off Boca Juniors and came to these shores with a reputation as a bit of a wild man. A gamble by Birmingham that came to an abrupt halt after just twenty-three games, when he jumped into the Saint Andrews crowd to silence a heckler! However, whilst Alberto is remembered fondly by the Birmingham fans, it was clearly a terrible piece of business. One crazy incident is recalled by a friend of my Uncle's, Tony Towers, who tells of when Birmingham played at Anfield. After the match a huge crowd stood waiting outside for Tarantini to grab his autograph. Sweet memories of the 1978 World cup were still fresh in supporter's minds and here amongst them was one of the heroes. As he came into sight, the Scousers surged forward to surround Alberto, but were shocked into silence as he began demanding £10 an autograph. Not surprisingly, this caused uproar amongst the crowd! Many started to insult an indignant Alberto and he ended up being dragged onto the team coach after wanting to fight them all! As for Manchester United, they retreated from Saint Andrews bruised, embarrassed, and with a manager under increasing pressure. Results and performances had to improve and fast for Dave Sexton, otherwise, like those before him he would be out.

(Elsewhere, Liverpool won 3-1 away at Queens Park Rangers, goals from Heighway, Kennedy and Johnson).

ACT FOURTEEN:
JONESTOWN, HELLO BAILEY AND SLOAN

Saturday 18th November 1978, should have meant nothing more to me than Ipswich Town at home, a chance to revenge our 3-0 thrashing that they handed out to us earlier on in the season. Also, an opportunity to wipe last's week's Birmingham City's 5-1 humiliation from our minds. Tragically, as I watched the television that day showing pictures of Jonestown in Guyana, even at such a tender age, I understood the full extent of the horror that occurred there. An American government congressman Republican Leo J. Ryan, and four other people investigating the Jim Jones cult were killed by members of the People's Temple. Greg Robinson, a SF Examiner photographer, Don Harris, NBC correspondent, Bob Brown, NBC cameraman and Patricia Parks, a Jonestown temple defector were shot down in cold blood. These initial killings were followed by a night of unflinching, merciless mass murder. 918 people were butchered at Jonestown, including 260 children. What always stuck with me was hearing of poor souls forced to drink a concoction of poison. Others shoved to the ground and injected with hypodermic syringes filled with cyanide and animal tranquilizer to kill them. The terrified people of Jonestown, some acceptant and serene through endless brainwashing, others scared out of their minds, probably coerced, queued to receive cups of "cyanide punch." The children were poisoned first and can be heard crying and wailing on the commune's own audio tapes that were later recovered by the FBI. When Guyanese troops finally reached Jonestown the next morning they discovered an eerie, silent landscape littered with the dead. There were a few survivors who had ran and hid whilst the slaughter was occurring. As for the maniac himself, Jones was found dead of an apparently self-inflicted gunshot. To this day, going back to watching on television all those years ago, Jonestown strangely fascinates and continues to haunt me.

Back to my first love of Manchester United.

Dave Sexton and me desperately needed a win. Our manager had finally seen the light and dropped Paddy Roche, who to be honest after the Birmingham game must have felt like he had faced a firing squad armed with machine guns for ninety minutes. Not able to endure much more Dave Sexton moved with the chequebook and agreed a deal with Coventry to buy their keeper Jim Blyth. Sexton spoke to the press telling them Paddy Roche's confidence had been shattered, not just by the Birmingham City result, but the lack of support he was getting from the fans. What did the man expect? Another own goal by the manager. Roche was turning young men's hair grey, and giving out heart palpitations on the United terraces. Not to mention amongst his own defenders. It simply couldn't go on. Alex Stepney was still at the club, but hadn't played a first game all season. Injured for too long a spell and clearly out of favour with the manager. There was Gary Bailey who appeared ready, but Sexton instead moved for Blyth. On hearing of his arrival to sign for United, the media scrum of the television, radio and press gathered at Old Trafford for the compulsory interviews and photographs-only to be shocked into silence when news emerged Jim Blyth had failed the medical. With Roche already told by Sexton that he was no longer his first choice, Stepney not even considered, the manager decided the kid from South Africa who paid his own fare for the opportunity to play for the club of his dreams would be handed an opportunity. So, into the goal came Gary Bailey and a lovely scenario introduced itself with him making his debut against Ipswich, Gary's Dad, Ray Bailey's club. Also, making a first start was nineteen-year-old Irish midfielder Tommy Sloan from Ballymena. After three home matches without a win at Old Trafford, United were under tremendous pressure to perform and perform they did. An early goal from Steve Coppell set the reds on their way against the cup holders and a 2-0 win was clinched late on as Jimmy Greenhoff struck to seal a much needed two points, but maybe equally important, United had turned up and played with a zeal and no shortage of style. As for the new boys, Bailey and Sloan, both had steady games and quietly impressed.

(Elsewhere, Liverpool won 1-0 at home against Manchester City, courtesy of a late Phil Neal penalty).

ACT FIFTEEN:
STALAGTITE AND STALAGNITES!

A final double lesson at school on a Tuesday, double geography, and who the hell was interested in stalactites and stalagmites? I wanted to know about different countries. Bolivia, where Butch and Sundance were gunned down. Texas, in the USA where the Alamo was. New York, New York, why did they name it twice? The capital of Peru? The beautiful long white sandy beaches of Rio De Janiero, full of kids playing football, not bloody stalactites and stalagmites upside down in caves. I was no fan of this form of geography, it bored me to tears. Finally, the bell rang for home time. I'd found a decent short cut that saved me having to walk down a packed Moston Lane. Instead, a more peaceful route through the Moston back streets that saw me home, chilled and ready for the reds. After tea and Grange Hill of course. That evening Manchester United travelled the short distance to Goodison Park where Gordon Lee's undefeated Everton were enjoying a fine season and hard on their neighbours Liverpool's heels. A charge led from the front by their prolific centre-forward Bob Latchford ably assisted by midfielder Andy King, with his many goals and assist. A stunning, recent winner against Liverpool in the Merseyside Derby already etched into Evertonian folklore, that being their first victory over Bob Paisley's team in seven years. Made even more incredible when the BBC tried interviewing King on the pitch at the final whistle, and a policeman angrily barged in and ordered them off. Obviously, a fed up Liverpool fan! As 42,126 watched on Everton blitzed United 3-0. Goals in the first-half from Trevor Ross and Andy King, followed by a third in the second from Bob Latchford. The reds were outplayed by a home side that had us on the back foot from the first minute. This defeat saw United drop to seventh and the mood swing on the terraces again turn badly against Sexton. This was Manchester United in name only. A shambles. Stalactites and bloody Stalagmites!

(Elsewhere, that evening, Liverpool drew 0-0 at Tottenham Hotspur).

ACT SIXTEEN:
CHALK AND CHEESE

A defeat too far for "Whispering Dave" as he'd been nicknamed in the newspapers, as Sexton immediately signed the twenty-four-year old Welsh international winger Mickey Thomas from Wrexham for £300,000. At last we had a proper number eleven again. Manchester United had been missing a top class left-sided winger since letting Gordon Hill go to Derby, but as footballers Merlin and Thomas were chalk and cheese. Hill was full of flair and tricks, audacious, a wonderful all-out attacking player, whilst Thomas? The prototype Sexton type footballer. Always prepared to help back if required, highly industrious, buzzing around, sharp and fast, always on the move. His debut arrived swiftly at Stamford Bridge against lowly Chelsea where Mickey posed beforehand for photographers in that simply wonderful, white with black and red trimmings tracksuit top. The chant from the United section as the teams warmed up:
"We all agree Manchester United are magic. We all agree Manchester City are tragic!" One of my early favourites!
A Chelsea side at the bottom of the table made a real game of it. Theirs' was a decent line up on paper that included the Wilkins brother Ray and Graham, winger Clive Walker and Duncan Mackenzie. As always appeared the case the lower side raised their game hugely against United and an entertaining first-half ensued that saw chances go astray for both teams. Slowly, as the second wore on the reds started to take control and on sixty-eight minutes, a sharp cut back from the line by Mickey Thomas was met by Jimmy Greenhoff's flashing header into the net. 1-0 the reds, and that's how it finished. A hard earned win and onto December where I hoped the real Manchester United would finally show itself.
(Elsewhere, Liverpool won 2-0 at home to Middleborough with goals from McDermott and Souness).

ACT SEVENTEEN:
BROKEN HEARTS AND BROKEN ARROWS

Saturday 9th December 1978.

It was the political winter of discontent, a Labour party at war with itself cutting their own throats. Prime Minister James Callaghan had lost the plot. Outraged Unions, scabs, picket lines, strikes, and some woman Tory MP called Margaret Thatcher just sat watching, smiling as the left tore itself apart-waiting to step in. It was a freezing, Mancunian December, the coldest on record since 1962-63. Boney M's ''Mary's Boy Child'' was number one in the charts, after taking over from Rod Stewart's ''Do you think I'm sexy.'' I still hated school and Manchester United were off to meet old friends in the East Midlands at Derby County's Baseball Ground. Thomas Henderson Docherty. Gordon Hill and Gerry Daly, former Old Trafford terrace heroes, especially Merlin, who was simply adored would line up against the reds who were giving eighteen-year-old Manchester born Andy Ritchie his debut, due to a Joe Jordan injury. There remained huge love for Tommy Doc who was given a hero's welcome by the travelling fans. A love Dave Sexton could only dream of. It turned out to be a truly entertaining match with Derby going in front after only three minutes when after the ball pinged around the United penalty area, Gerry Daly fired low past Gary Bailey from eight yards out. A delighted Daly was swiftly mobbed and first to him was a beaming Gordon Hill. Both left Old Trafford under a cloud of bad feelings regarding their relationship with Dave Sexton and this was clearly payback time. Shortly after Hill smashed in a ferocious thirty-yard drive that Bailey was happy to tip over the Bar. Beware former lovers who come armed with broken hearts and broken arrows. It was end to end action that had the crowd baying-United hit back with Mickey Thomas flashing in a cracking twenty-yard shot superbly saved by Derby keeper Colin Boulton. On thirty-minutes we got a deserved equaliser and it was the new boy who after wonderful approach play by Jimmy Greenhoff and Mickey Thomas, Andy Ritchie shot low and his effort rolled under Boulton into the net. Just to be sure Sammy McIlroy helped the ball over the line, but the glory clearly belonged to Ritchie. Two disallowed goals swiftly followed, firstly, Lou Macari's from a corner after it was alleged Gordon McQueen pushed his marker, followed by Sammy McIlroy who was deemed to be offside. With the reds continually pushing forward, it was no surprise when right on half-time from a McIlroy free kick, Jimmy Greenhoff smashed low past Boulton after a mix up in the Derby defence. United at times resembled the Doc's team of old, no more so than on fifty three-minutes when Gordon Hill of all players lost possession and the reds flew away on a thrilling counter attack. Racing down the left wing Jimmy Greenhoff tore onwards before crossing perfectly for Andy Ritchie to head home. Two goals on his debut, 3-1, and game over.

(Elsewhere, at Anfield, Liverpool beat the champions Nottingham Forest 2-0, with a brace from McDermott. Ending their astonishing, record beating forty two games unbeaten run).

ACT EIGHTEEN:
"I COULD CRY NOW"

Saturday 16th December 1978. Christmas was getting closer with
Manchester United in sixth spot. We'd already seen a game at
Norwich postponed as the weather cut deep and next up were
Tottenham Hotspur at Old Trafford. 52,026 were present hoping
United could continue their recent good form. Andy Ritchie kept his
place up front alongside the evergreen thirty-two-year-old Jimmy
Greenhoff, and once more the two clicked as the reds won 2-0. Goals
from Sammy McIlroy and Ritchie securing the points. In the visitor's
midfield that day were two beautiful footballing artists. One born in
Hayes, East London, the other, Cordoba, Argentina. Glenn Hoddle
and Osvaldo Ardiles. Yet, our boys ran all over them like red army
ants. It was Sexton football, high pressure. Attack, but always with
more than a modicum of caution. Some may call it grown-up football,
but those with a United soul still yearned for more, they missed the
doc's angel dust. Suddenly, as the full time whistle sounded
Manchester United were only five points behind Liverpool. Whilst
recording this in my MUFC OK notepad, the realisation hit home that
if we beat them at Old Trafford on Boxing Day, a title chase was truly
on. How had this happened after the ups and downs of this season?
My heart told me to be prepared for glory, our first title since 1967.
My head agreed also for Christmas time was coming into sight, and
truly wonderful things happen at Christmas. No school for two weeks,
no idiot bullies, no boring maths, geography, woodwork or practical
(waste of time) Studies). It would just be so nice being at home,
searching for my Christmas presents. Mum and dad were becoming
wise, but not wise enough. Whilst at nan and grandad's in Penn
Street, I discovered on my travels a World Cup Subbuteo Edition
hidden on top of their bedroom wardrobe. Unwrapped, I daren't touch
it, but on my tip toes I could just about make out Pele. I could cry
now thinking about it. "Where is he?" I hear a voice downstairs say.
"What's he bloody up to?" The sheer joy and excitement. The

amount of times I sneaked off when round there just to stare at it. Also, not forgetting time planning Crofton United's glorious future with Captain Jackie and enjoying my expanding music collection. These included Grease and A Bridge Too Far movie soundtracks and a 45 single of Rolf Harris singing ''Football Crazy.'' Whatever happened to him? Listening to Radio Two's, the News Huddlines with Roy Hudd. Saturday afternoon at One o'clock, I so loved that show. Followed by Jim Rosenthal introducing Sport on 2. Most importantly though I had my reds and three huge games coming up against Bolton Wanderers away, Liverpool and West Bromwich Albion at home. The Christmas tree was up, the festive songs were all over the air waves, we even had Carol singers on our road. What could possibly go wrong?

(Elsewhere, Liverpool lost 1-0 at Bristol City to a Joe Royle goal, and suddenly I began to believe in Father Christmas once more).

ACT NINETEEN:
"BRING ME SUNSHINE!"

Friday 22nd December 1978.
Bolton Wanderers 3 Manchester United 0.
On the cover of our Christmas TV Times was a photograph of Sean
Connery as James Bond with Morecambe and Wise either side of him
holding guns. These three would've proved more of a threat up front
for the reds as we were humiliated at Burnden Park. There was
actually a Bolton fan in our class at school who was an idiot, so small
mercies our Christmas holidays had started and I wouldn't have to
face him for a while. One man stood out like a prince amongst
footballing paupers on the snowy, ice-bound, bumpy pitch that
evening under the Burnden floodlights. The charismatic Elvis Presley
adoring, footballing magician, the one and only Frank Worthington.
"United should sign him," said Dad, often. "A proper United
player." Inspirational, deadly in front of goal and blessed with that
littler extra magic known these days as box office. Worthington's two
goals and a third from former United player Alan Gowling left the
Bolton fans ecstatic, their Christmas presents arriving three days
early. Other ex-reds in their line up included Tommy Docherty's
biggest fan Willie Morgan, at that time involved in a bitter court battle
with his old boss and just to rub the result in even further, thirty-
seven-year-old full back Tony Dunne. Never forgetting the manager
Ian greaves. A bitter rivalry existed (still does) between the two sets
of fans stemming from the post Munich air disaster. After beating a
decimated Manchester United 2-0 in the 1958 FA Cup final, the
Wanderers team bus decided to begin their parade thirteen-miles from
home country in of all places Salford's, Irlam on the Heights. A
burning United hotspot of support. Emotions were still red raw after
Munich and the bus at first sight came under attack from both sides of
the road as stones, bricks, flour, fruit, beer, tomatoes, whatever came
to hand was launched. Nat Lofthouse's vicious challenge on Harry

Gregg had left a bad taste in United supporter's mouths, and was returned with bells on. "It was like bloody Cheyenne country!" exclaimed a Bolton director who was on the bus. More like the Salford Sioux. Making his debut for Manchester United at left-back that day in place of an injured Stewart Houston was twenty-one year-old from Newry, Northern Ireland, Tom Connell. It could only get easier for Tom who wasn't by any means our worst player that day. Next up a date with a team I dreaded more than any other. Liverpool.

ACT TWENTY:
CRUCIFIX AND GARLIC

Boxing day. Tuesday 26th December 1978.

 Santa hadn't let me down!

The World Cup Subbuteo Edition was finally officially revealed in all its glory and pomp and I really had to congratulate myself on my acting performance on first viewing. I'm pretty sure mum and dad never fell for it though. Despite the beauty of new presents, Christmas treats such as first time movies on television and special festive radio shows, come Boxing Day everything was centred around one grand occasion. My reds were at home to a team I feared only a little less than the Hammer House of Horror films. Christopher Lee and Peter Cushing with their vampire adventures on a late Friday evening, always making me ensure the windows was shut, and desperately searching for a crucifix and garlic! As for that other horror, Liverpool, the fact they hadn't scored on their last five visits to Old Trafford offered a little hope, plus it was Christmas-and as everyone knew wonderful things happened at…already tried that. Desperation, you see.

Manchester United 0 Liverpool 3.

We were lucky to get away with just 3. It was a footballing masterclass from Bob Paisley's team. The ordeal began with a fine Ray Kennedy header finishing off a great move followed up by a Jimmy Case drive past a helpless Gary Bailey on twenty-five minutes. Between the goals United struggled to even get near the ball as a rampant Liverpool mastered by the wonderful passing, probing and sheer strutting arrogance of Graeme Souness-allied to Kenny Dalglish's cunning and guile took apart Sexton's willing, hard running, but hugely outclassed team apart. It was total football separated not by a handful of points, but different worlds. Their players so comfortable in possession. Pass and move, small triangles, the ball moved effortlessly across the Old Trafford pitch as red shirts attempted with little joy to hunt them down. Two years previous we stopped Liverpool achieving a historic treble beating them at Wembley in the FA Cup. Against them United had always found a way to rise to the occasion, not on that day. Men against boys. 54,910 watched on in dismay and I dare say grudging respect for a truly magnificent team. Whether it be festive spirit or just sheer admiration for witnessing a beautiful goal, it was a rare day indeed when a Manchester United crowd applauded a Liverpool goal at Old Trafford. This occurred on sixty-seven minutes with the Scousers 2-0 up, full of swagger and verve and enjoying putting their most ferocious rivals to the sword. The player famously labelled "Super sub" David Fairclough had made a rare start and how he made the most of this when leaving four United player in his blistering wake, before the red-flamed hair attacker flicked the ball over Gary Bailey into an empty net. As jubilant visiting supporters celebrated, applause also began to break out across other parts of the stadium for Fairclough's audacious and breath-taking goal. "They're as good as anything in Europe," admitted a shell-shocked Dave Sexton afterwards. "And a certainty to win the League." United were due to play Liverpool once more in the return League game at Anfield in April. However, the FA Cup was drawing close, if the unthinkable occurred, I could only pray for the spirit of 77 to return and maybe arm myself with a crucifix and plenty of garlic.

ACT TWENTY ONE:
THE BEAUTY AND THE BEAST

Saturday 30th December 1978. They say you always remember your
first time, well mine is enshrined in my head, every single, last
moment of it. I was going to the match! Dad had bought tickets for
the forthcoming home game against West Bromwich Albion at Old
Trafford and the fact we were in the midst of a bus strike wasn't going
to stop us as we hitched a lift with one of his mates-and he was
picking us up too. Once dropped off at the top of Warwick Road, we
joined the supporters wrapped up from head to toe in new United
Christmas hats and scarves trying to fight off the absolutely, freezing
weather. A sea of red, white and black, we made our way towards the
ground. I tucked my new United scarf around my neck. "Pull your zip
up on your coat J," said dad. I recognised immediately mum's voice
telling him: "Make sure he stays wrapped up Johnny!" I looked up
staring at the floodlights. I was hypnotised. It was still only
two- thirty in the afternoon, but dark skies were swiftly gathering
overhead and a shower of snowflakes had begun to fall. My dad
grabbed my hand: "Come on, let's get inside." Walking fast over the
bridge I spotted "THE END IS NIGH" man with his banner appear in
front of us. "Already happened against the Scousers mate!" I heard
someone shout over towards him. "Now fuck off!" Charming, I
thought, but he had a point. A packed forecourt, two Police horses
patrolling: huge black creatures stomping angrily with grim-faced
officers pulling on their reins. Ticket touts on the lookout for
customers. "Anybody want tickets?!" The smell of burger and chips.
Grease oil, and onions. "Glory, Glory Man United!" roared out, fists
in the air from a gang of lads nearby. It was intoxicating, real, It was
Old Trafford. I looked up and there read the words.
Manchester United Football Club.
I caught my breath and grabbed Dad's hand tighter. As we walked
across to the K Stand turnstiles, I busied myself listening in to fellow

reds nearby. "I'd rather have Kermit the fuckin' frog than Sexton, Bob," one bloke let it be known to his mate who nodded in agreement. "I'd make do with Miss fuckin' Piggy, Jim," he replied. Dave Sexton appeared the main source of conversation amongst the fans and I had the feeling not many had sent him a Christmas card. "We're gonna get bloody hammered by this lot today," I heard someone else exclaim loud. I had to admit the thought had crossed my mind. West Brom were riding high in the League and their impressive new manager Ron Atkinson in his first full season at the helm had put together a side full of pace, power and guile. None more than their three black players nicknamed by the newspapers: "The Three Degrees". Defender Brendan Batson, forwards Cyril Regis and Laurie Cunningham. Back then in the dying embers of 1978, the world was a totally different place when it came to the colour of someone's skin. The stuff I heard, if spoken, shouted or sung today would infuriate, and cause public outrage. Those times a banana being thrown on the pitch and monkey chants aimed in their direction was a regular occurrence for Batson, Regis and Cunningham. Sadly, Old Trafford that day would shame itself. "What shocked me when I joined West Brom was the volume," recalled Batson. "The noise and level of the abuse was incredible. At times, it was almost like surround sound in the grounds. But it was such a regular occurrence you almost got used to it." Our crowd that day was no different.
It was just England...
 After queuing for a small period we headed inside the ground. Dad bought me a programme, (I still have it) treated himself to a pint, me an orange juice and a bag of crisp. I looked again at our ticket stubs counting out the different set of small steps that led up into the stadium before figuring out which one was ours. I heard the tannoy playing Boney M. I was so sick of that song! I listened to the faint hub of the crowd already in their seats. The first "United!" from the direction of The Stretford End began. Finally, we headed up, I went first, dad did that on purpose, I know that now. The last step before you enter and then, then you see it. You rub your eyes; your mouth is wide open. The pitch, the huge grandstands rapidly filling. It's simply

all too much to take in-then an arm on your shoulder: "Come on, let's go sit down." We took our seats, what a view. Dad disappeared back downstairs and returned with two steaming hot Bovril's. Five minutes to Three o'clock, I so could have got used to this. 45,091, now waiting eagerly, finally the teams appeared from the tunnel. They broke to warm up, the line ups were announced, my heart was beating loud as the snow started to fall just that little bit more and colder. Maybe a warning of what was set to occur.

THE TEAMS

Manchester United. Bailey, Houston, B Greenhoff, Buchan, McQueen, Coppell, McIlroy, McCreery, Thomas, J Greenhoff and Ritchie.

West Bromwich Albion. Godden, Batson, Wile, Robertson, Statham, T Brown, Robson, Cantello, Cunningham, A Brown and Regis.

Little did anyone know we were on the cusp of watching greatness unfurl as one of the finest games of football in the history of the English game was set to begin. After our last two 3-0 drubbings, few had little doubt of United turning up against West Brom but would that be enough? Well, in a stunning first-half the reds were forced into playing some of their best football of the season, just to stay in the game. Similar to Tommy Docherty's Manchester United, Ron Atkinson's West Brom attacked home and away, going close early on with a Batson header from a free kick by their dynamic young midfielder-the curly haired Geordie Bryan Robson. Later, so gloriously of this Parish. United hit back with Brian Greenhoff smashing in a shot that Tony Gooden was forced to tip over. From the following McIlroy corner, the ball fell again to the same Greenhoff, who this time smashed home a twenty-yard, looping volley past Gooden! Twenty one minutes gone as Old Trafford erupted and it appeared United were determined to put the ghosts of their recent Christmas past behind them. Seven minutes later it was 1-1-with the rancid abuse ringing loud, Laurie Cunningham began a wonderful move with a pass to Robson, whose quick thinking let in Tony Brown to hammer an equaliser past Gary Bailey. The vile chants to West Brom's three black players didn't just occur on the field of play, it came from hate mail also. Laurie Cunningham suffered most through his on account of having a well publicised white fiancée called Nicky White. His teammate and good friend Bryan Robson remembers himself being sent disgusting letters asking him how an Englishman could tolerate having black team-mates? The club itself would often receive bile through the post off an Everton fan who directed his garbage at the manager, urging Atkinson not to select his "monkeys" for any games at Goodison.

As the game restarted heavy torrents of snow began falling down and under the beautiful, dreamy haze of the Old Trafford floodlights, Laurie Cunningham was at it again! Here at the theatre of past-dreams, Laurie was performing already on an Old Trafford stage perfect for his dazzling talents, despite many in the audience simply too pig ignorant to see beyond the colour of skin. The gathering snow, and mud patches on the ice bound surface appeared irrelevant to Cunningham, as he slalomed, danced and floated across the pitch with the ball chased by desperate red shirts, before finally finding Cyril Regis-whose back flick fed Len Cantello to crash a fantastic shot high past Bailey into the net. Two stunning goals in as many minutes by West Brom swiftly delivered me back to reality, as I envisaged yet another good hiding. "At least we scored a goal dad," I said trying to raise his spirits. By this time my hood was on, scarf over mouth as nothing short of a blizzard swept across the stadium. Inside, despite my undying loyalty to the reds a little piece of me had already fallen in love with this West Brom team, but these were trying times, my lot needed me more. Three minutes later on the half-hour United were level-a leaping Gordon McQueen smashing a header past Gooden from a Sammy McIlroy free kick. 2-2: It was incredible stuff! I watched on as these dramatic events unfolded thinking was it always like this? I knew better, but before I could catch my breath, Steve Coppell robbed their defender Derek Statham and set up a fired-up McIlroy, who took on the visiting defence, dribbled past one then two, before letting fly into the bottom corner! 3-2 the reds, and what the hell was going on?! The action continued at a frantic pace and right on half-time, Tony Brown scored his second by poking the ball home past an onrushing Gary Bailey, after Cantello set him up. 3-3! Born close by in nearby Wythenshawe, it was no surprise reading in the programme that Tony Brown was raised a United fan. Didn't stop him though did it-both teams received a standing ovation at the interval as they left the pitch. In later years Ron Atkinson recalled an embarrassing moment of missing that last goal. "I went into the dressing room and told the lads that they didn't deserve to be losing 3-2, and that there was no reason in the world why we shouldn't grab an equaliser. They all just sat there and looked at me like I was mad! Then, Tony Brown said: "Boss, what are you on about, it's 3-3. I've just equalised!"

"Bomber had just run through and put the ball in at the Stretford End, but I'd heard a whistle blow and thought it was half-time? Then, there he is staring at me as if I had just lost my marbles. So, I just told them: "Well, fair enough. Go and get me a winner then!"

The second-half saw West Brom appear determined to give their manager what he desired. None more than Laurie Cunningham-a sight to behold in full flow. So magical to watch, almost as if Laurie left no footprints in the snow such was the grace and speed he moved with the ball at his feet. Alongside Cyril Regis, all tremendous power and thunderous pace terrorising the United centre-halves, the visitors swarmed forward. There followed two stunning all-out saves from Gary Bailey as he become involved in a personal duel with Cyril Regis. Both times forced to fly right across his goal mouth to stop Regis's long range, stinging efforts. Brian Greenhoff was also forced to deny him with a clearance off the line. By now it felt like a procession, just a matter of time before the inevitable occurred. Regis put Cunningham away soaring into the penalty area, where Stewart Houston's attempt to stop the winger was akin to Ron Harris all those years ago trying to hack down George Best, only to taste wind in his mouth and in Houston's case, ice and snow. On went Cunningham, the monkey chants so loud before he buried a superb shot past Bailey. All this achieved with the ease of an enchanting young footballer who loved to dance and dance, he left bereft United defenders slipping, sliding and utterly hopeless to stop him. The abuse stopped momentarily, but it would start again and be picked up on the monitor by ITV commentator Gerald Sinstadt.

Back home in Birmingham, Laurie Cunningham shared a house with fellow player West Brom player Alastair Brown. "Death threats were posted to our house. On one occasion a petrol bomb was thrown through the front door. Another time, I can recall Laurie calmly stamping out the flames licking at the doormat, as if it were the sort of thing that happened every day. His only recourse remained on the pitch. That season more than any other, Laurie was able to keep striking back and winning games."

Saving the best for last, West Bromwich Albion completed their tour de force performance with a truly glorious fifth. Once more defying the garbage, rancid comments being hurled off the Old Trafford terraces, Laurie Cunningham exploded from his own half down the right hand touchline to leave a breathless Stewart Houston behind, appearing close to exhaustion. They could rage, make ape grunts, do monkey gestures, it made no difference for Laurie raced away with a swagger and his beloved funk music roaring loud drowning out the bigots. Accelerating into United's half, he found Tony Brown-the deft touch to an incoming storm called Cyril Regis, who let fly an instant shot past a bewildered Gary Bailey that he never had a chance in hell of getting near. A crowning moment for the visitors to leave the score a now legendary Manchester United 3 West Bromwich Albion 5.

In the Mancunian snow and ice.

Post-match. In the interviews for the ITV Kick Off programme, when asked by Gerald Sinstadt who was his man of the match, Dave Sexton answered with bleeding red eyes: "Steve Coppell." When Ron

Atkinson was asked for his reply it spoke volumes for the times. "That would be a toss-up between one of the coloured front people." They say the past is a distant country, let's hope it stays that way when it comes to racism. For my opening game it truly was a case of Beauty and the Beast. There were wonderful moments that I'll treasure, impossible not to. You never forget that first time with your dad. A rites of passage. Sadly, the abuse hurled at the black players stayed with me too. How could it not?

ACT TWENTY TWO:
"EVERYBODY OUT!"

The Sun paper headline was "Crisis? What Crisis?"
As UK Prime Minister James Callaghan denied that the country was in chaos during the line ripped straight from Richard 111, "The Winter of Discontent". Strikes, strikes, government strife, the country in political turmoil and what's more I'd lost my football. January was a month where there were only twelve First Division league games played due to severe weather conditions. It was a drab and dreary dark, miserable opening to 1979, but at least there was the start of the FA Cup and we'd drawn Chelsea at home in the Third Round. The way United were performing beggars couldn't afford to be choosers, so, after the worst Christmas of my eleven years on this planet, life finally got a little more back to normal when on Monday 15th January 1979, the football returned. These were worrying times for Dave Sexton, with only 38,743, turning up at Old Trafford to see the reds take on Chelsea. One thing was certain to galvanise Louis Edwards and the Manchester United boardroom into action regarding a change of manager-running off with the physio's wife apart, and that was a loss of finance due to empty seats in the stadium. With it being on a Monday evening, lousy weather, picket lines, shouts of "Everybody out!" a daily event and I'm not talking about United's kamikaze offside system. Prevailing chaos in the workplaces and high streets, but mitigating circumstances aside supporters weren't showing because the football United churned out wasn't good enough. It was dull beyond belief. Sexton was coming under extreme pressure from the newspapers, and on the terraces. A good run in the FA Cup was now deemed an absolute necessity, if this quiet, decent but fiercely under-fire manager wished to keep his job.
Luckily, Sexton's old team turned up at Old Trafford with a concoction of old veterans (Ron Harris and Peter Osgood), kids making first team debuts and without their impressive and influential

Captain Ray ''Butch'' Wilkins. With Chelsea nailed to the bottom of the First Division table also it came as little surprise, except to me probably that United despatched them with consummate ease 3-0. A first half goal from Steve Coppell, plus two more from Jimmy Greenhoff and Ashley Grimes after the interval eased United through. A real plus for the reds was a return for the long standing injured Stuart Pearson in his first appearance of the season, after a terrible knee injury. Pancho received a warm welcome from the Old Trafford crowd, a real hero of what felt like by then a long, gone age. The Docherty era. Come the following summer Stuart Pearson would depart for pastures new at West Ham United, but his time in our colours would never be forgotten.

(Elsewhere, two days later, Liverpool beat Southend 3-0 in the FA Cup, with goals from Case, Dalglish and Kennedy).

ACT TWENTY THREE:
I DON'T LIKE MONDAYS

Your stomach is in knots.
Trying to fall asleep on a Sunday night when it was school in the morning, you're tossing and turning, listening to far off noises. Distant trains, traffic hum. Dreading, utterly dreading that drifting of first light into the bedroom through the window to signal a whole week beginning again. The time arrives, you pull the sheets back and simply go into autopilot. Keep the dreaming in your head. No one can get in there. Living by numbers, Math's, first two, and I never had the slightest idea what he was going on about. Tell me why I don't like Mondays? I wasn't too keen on Tuesday, Wednesday, Thursday and Friday either. Still, at least I had my reds, midweek away to Fulham in the Fourth Round of the FA Cup. One lesson, day at a time eh?

The shooting occurred on Monday 29th January 1979, at a public elementary school in San Diego, California, United States. The principal and a custodian were killed, plus eight children and a police officer injured. A sixteen-year-old girl Brenda Spencer, who lived in a house across the street from the school was convicted of the shootings. Charged as an adult she pleaded guilty to two counts of murder and assault with a deadly weapon. Spencer was given an indefinite sentence. A reporter reached her by phone while she was still in the house after the shooting and asked why she had done it? "I don't like Mondays," she replied. Boom! Bob got his song. Our cup runneth on and two days after, Wednesday 31st January 1979, in front of 25,229, Manchester United fought out a thrilling, if gruelling 1-1 draw with Bobby Campbell's Second Division Fulham. The first-half saw the reds come under tremendous pressure from the home side with Gary Bailey forced into making three terrific saves. None more so than against one time Arsenal wonder kid Peter

Marinello, who at times tore United to shreds. Finally, we woke up and five minutes before half time, Stuart Pearson crossed wonderfully for Jimmy Greenhoff to smash low a stunning volley into the net. The old partnership working in tandem once more. Still Fulham attack after the interval deservedly grabbing an equaliser on the hour when a glorious header from John Margerrison beats Bailey to flash into the top corner. Come the final whistle a draw was more than a fair result, but a sad epitaph of this night at the Cottage was seeing Stuart Pearson stretchered off late on after being injured once more. He would never play for Manchester United again. The raised fist from the elbow after scoring against Liverpool in the 1977 FA Cup Final, remembered forever by the red army. Cheers Pancho.
(Elsewhere, Liverpool beat Blackburn 1-0 in the FA Cup at Anfield, with a goal from Dalglish).

ACT TWENTY FOUR:
SAME OLD

Four days later the reds were back on their knees.
Saturday 3rd February 1979. Manchester United 0 Arsenal 2, and
45,460, watched on dismally at Old Trafford as a Gunners team
inspired by their bewitching, midfield genius Liam Brady tore United
apart in the first-half whenever the mood took him. It swiftly became
apparent that after three League defeats on the row Dave Sexton's
instructions to the team was to not concede. To the angst and
frustration of the crowd we shuffled endlessly back in obviously,
rehearsed drills, but many a time it was to no avail as Brady with a
swish of that magical left foot found holes that other players simply
could never see. It should have been over at the interval as Arsenal
created but missed several good opportunities. They just kept going-a
swift throw out from Pat Jennings set Liam Brady off as he swept
down United's right-hand side of the pitch, teasing red shirts before
letting fly with a shot that Bailey just managed to tip aside. Still they
came, Alan Sunderland from ten-yards out with just Bailey to beat
smashed high over the bar. One minute later Sunderland once more
tried to chip the United keeper only for the ball to fly just wide.
United tried hard following the interval to fight back but the Gunner's
centre half pairing of Willie Young and David O'Leary always had
the edge over a misfiring Jimmy Greenhoff, who badly missed his
strike partner, the injured Joe Jordan. With Macari, McIlroy and
Thomas, all but anonymous, the yellow shirts of Arsenal continued to
run riot. Rix fired in a shot from twenty-yards that Bailey pushed
away and from the resulting corner, Young's header flew inches wide.
On a rare United break Steve Coppell set up a raiding Stewart
Houston who shot haplessly over the bar to the rising anger of the
fans. Houston was swiftly becoming a scapegoat as his own
performances started to fall off a cliff. Arsenal swept forward again-
on sixty-four minutes Rix's cross found David Price at the far post,
whose header back was swept in by Sunderland from close range. As

the Old Trafford crowd tried their best to rouse the team Brady took possession weaving his way through before finding his Captain Pat Rice, whose sliding pass to Alan Sunderland dissected United's defence. Taking aim the Arsenal forward smashed low past Gary Bailey. 2-0. Same old, the reds were already well beaten just past the hour. Intent on making matters infinitely worst the sublime Brady split us open for the umpteenth time finding a hat-trick seeking Sunderland, who fired in a shot that rattled Gary Bailey's post. Still, the yellow shirted Londoners wouldn't leave well alone, seemingly determined to grind Manchester United noses into the mud, dirt, and the odd remaining blade of grass of our famous old stadium. Come full-time they hadn't managed to add anymore, but done enough to inflict considerable damage on Dave Sexton and his seriously out of form team. The red army across the stadium were no longer just bored, they seethed, venting their collective spleen on the manager. It was hard to take and to see such a gorgeous talent as the Dublin born twenty-three-year-old Liam Brady in the skin. Where was our Brady? To them Sexton was building a team of robots. Old Trafford was a home to heroes, a field of footballing beauty and imagination. Edwards, Crerand, Charlton, Best and Law. Not for the Manchester United crowd a side whose main aim from kick off appeared not to be chase dreams and glory, but don't get beat. As for the man whose goals destroyed us, the curly permed-hair deadly Alan Sunderland, well, good riddance for the season. I'd had more than enough of him. My MUFC OK notepad was nothing short of a Shakespearean tragedy. Most pages etched with tears. A little dramatic maybe, but not far off the truth. The reds had now lost four consecutive League matches and next up a team in blue from down the road. Moss Side and the Derby was calling, as was my birthday.
(Elsewhere, Liverpool beat West Brom 2-1, in a top of the table clash at Anfield, with goals from Dalglish and Fairclough).

ACT TWENTY FIVE:
OUR FATHER'S AND HOLY MARY'S

To this day ninety per cent of the birthday cards I receive has a football on the front, the other ten, a pint of beer or a glass of wine. Back in 79, they all had footballs.

Once I had escaped from School on Friday, all thoughts turned immediately not to what presents I was going to get for my birthday on the Sunday, but just to which United team would turn up at Maine Road on the Saturday. Across the great Manchester divide back in January, City relieved their manager Tony Book of first team duties to bring back Malcom "Big Mal" Allison, his cigars and sheepskin coats after five years away to try and reignite the glory days of the late sixties, early seventies. Book was kept on to work with Allison, whose immediate impression of his chairman Peter Swales was quite remarkable. "I looked at him, saw the comb-over, the England blazer, the suede shoes, and thought this isn't going to work." Big Mal's initial impact was hilarious as City were beaten 2-0 and knocked out of the FA Cup at fourth division minnows Shrewsbury Town. Much to my and every other local red's delight. You couldn't find a blue that day with binoculars and a team of huskies. Sadly, the old magic finally clicked for Allison with a 3-0 victory at Spurs which meant after some terrible form City were going into the Derby with renewed confidence thinking they could continue our pain, and in doing so ruin my birthday. Blue mates and wingers from Crofton United, Hilly and Ashy would be at Maine Road. Not just simply Junior Blues, they even took turns at ball boy duty. In United terms, I couldn't think of two worse. We'd have been better off with Mike Summerbee and Mike Doyle in my opinion. The old stomach churning returned, all week Allison had been mouthing in the newspapers how he, they were going to destroy United, but Dave Sexton never bit, he simply wasn't the type. This remained a huge part of the problem regarding the United supporter's relationship with Sexton, for they had become accustomed to Tommy Docherty's showbusiness approach to press conferences and interviews. Everyone an occasion you could sell tickets for (he probably tried), as for the journalists it became more of what to leave out, such was the abundance of interesting and funny quotes. Whereas Sexton, the well, if not dry was only ever hardly a quarter full and even that was tepid. There was never any jokes, gossip off the record but you could print it anyway, unlike the Doc who left hacks hanging on his every word, Sexton bored, annoyed and ultimately left them utterly frustrated struggling for any decent copy. Thus, came the slings, arrows, slurs, personal insults and hurtful back page headlines off the tabloid newspapers.

So, come Saturday 10th February 1979, and 46,151 filled Maine Road. As ever reds were everywhere inside the ground when it came to this fixture and on a sandpit of a pitch, United took the day 3-0!
 Two from Steve Coppell, his second one of the goals of the season and a thumping volleyed third from the red's best player that day, Andy Ritchie, saw City fans leaving well before the final whistle-such had been United's dominance. In typical, brainstorming fashion Malcom Allison employed Colin Bell as a sweeper, but Sexton's ploy of having the mobile and elusive Ritchie play on him rendered this a disastrous move, totally confusing the other City defenders. United played their best football for months sweeping forward in waves. Sammy McIlroy the first flashing in a shot over the bar-still we attacked, McIlroy again striding through the City defence into the penalty area, and as Joe Corrigan rushed towards him Sammy hooked the ball over for Steve Coppell to control on his chest before firing past three blue shirts and a desperately, diving Corrigan into the far corner. Like the rest of his defence Corrigan was performing with a nervousness stemming from Allison's over complicated tactics, and there was much worse to come for them. Appearing a team reborn, the slick reds moved the ball around fast and accurate on a surface even Blackpool donkeys would have took exception too, and ten minutes from half-time Jimmy Greenhoff crafted a wonderfully,

ncisive pass to free Steve Coppell, who let fly a magnificent right
'ooted shot that flew past Corrigan into the top corner. It was a
stunning goal shocking all in the stadium, such had been Coppell's
echnique and crashing finish. Half-time arrived, and the cheers of the
Jnited supporters erupted from across the ground. The main legions
hough dancing and singing in one huge corner around and on top of a
'iccadilly Radio billboard set on a tunnel. Come the start of the
second-half, no doubt their ears stinging from a Malcom Allison
earful, City woke up putting the reds on the backfoot. Brian
Greenhoff not helping the cause when a ridiculous back pass let in
Brian Kidd, only for him to be foiled at the last by Gary Bailey. The
game swung both ways, but it was United having by far the best of the
chances. Red shirts fighting, throwing themselves into tackles,
Mickey Thomas in the thick of it. More importantly when the time
came playing swift, impressive attacking football, summed up
perfectly on sixty-nine minutes, when from a McIlroy deflection, after
some fine approach play the eighteen-year-old Andy Ritchie on his
Derby debut slammed home a ferocious volley past Corrigan to
decide the match-bragging rights. 3-0, and as the red army sang:
'Oh when the reds come marching in!'' the city punters fans started
o depart in droves. It was no more than Sexton's team deserved-the
'ans delighted, recent dreadful results were duly forgiven for great
deeds in Derby games cover a multitude of past sins. In Catholic
erms imagine Confession, telling all and coming clean, (well almost
all), receiving nothing more than a handful of Our Father's and Holy
Mary's for penance, and you were then in the clear. Amen!
As the final whistle sounded there appeared more reds than blues left
n the ground. A result for Dave Sexton arriving like a lighthouse in a
storm. Maybe there was hope yet for the quiet man this season,
maybe? As for my twelfth birthday, the following day I can't honestly
remember what I got, no doubt mostly football related-United, but my
best present had already been penned and duly noted for posterity and
piss taking in the MUFC OK notepad.
Manchester City 0 Manchester United 3!
Twelve years old now. I was getting on a bit.

It was tense later that evening at Gill Woods newsagents as we waited for the Football Pink's arrival. It didn't do to take the piss if one or the other had been beaten, an unwritten rule, so an air of respect filled the air. I so wanted to start singing "3-0!" but daren't, I would have been put through the shop window. I simply nodded my head in agreement with all that was being said. "Fuckin' Allison hasn't got a clue!" moaned a blue.

"Sexton still has it all to prove," replied a red, to which everyone grunted and nodded their heads. Me included. Finally, thank God, the Football Pinks came rushing into the shop and to read it all, twice, have to admit, I took the long way home…

(Elsewhere, Liverpool beat Birmingham City 1-0 at Anfield, with a goal from Souness).

ACT TWENTY SIX:
AVON CALLING

Two days on from the Maine Road Derby, Manchester United were back in action at Old Trafford against Fulham in an FA Cup Fourth Round replay. 41,200 turned up to see the reds finally see off Bobby Campbell's team with a Jimmy Greenhoff goal midway through the second half to avoid extra time. Jimmy's thirteenth of the season. Gold dust. Again, Fulham came to play and it was a relieved Old Trafford crowd who were happy to hear the final whistle. Earlier that same Monday, I had managed to scrape a day off school, (no way was any bastard going to ruin my recent good times). It was the Fifth Round draw from the Football Association at Lancaster House. The rattling of the balls going into the velvet bag, the great expectation of who we were going to play-please God not Liverpool. Between drinking Lucozade, playing Subbuteo and painting my Africa Korps Airfix soldiers, I listened out for the reds.

''Colchester City.''

Then more rummaging of the balls.

''Will play Manchester United!''

Yes! We would be away to Third Division Colchester City. Rather them than an away game at Anfield, the City Ground or Highbury. At my ripe old of twelve already the romantic in me was starting to vanish and I was becoming practical. I wanted to see my team at Wembley, let's save the monsters for later on in the competition.

Tuesday 20th February 1979. 7.20, BBC1. Blake's Seven. On the planet Fosforon, Avon tries to persuade an old friend to hand over a vital component in the latest Federation cypher machine. On the Liberator, Blake and the others watch as an Earth ship listed as missing centuries earlier approaches the planet. Meanwhile, back in my bedroom, I listened on the radio to Manchester United take on Colchester at Layer Road with nerves shredded as the home team sounded all over us. There was mad penalty area scrambles, red shirted defenders falling over, a disallowed goal and off the line clearances. Gary Bailey was working overtime as a gathered crowd of 13,171, most of them full of under-dog bluster and blood lust, screaming for a Cup upset and to ruin my life. Thankfully, the reds hung on becoming increasingly dangerous as the clock ticked down. Class eventually told when with just four minutes remaining, it was that man again Jimmy Greenhoff swooping from a corner at the far post, after an Andy Ritchie flick on to put Manchester United into the Quarter-Finals! Wembley was within sight; Dave Sexton's soldiers were marching on. The FA Cup had become everything. A kind draw, a fair wind and a few prayers into the ear of Saint Dunstan across the road could swing it, for everybody loved the reds. Didn't they?

ACT TWENTY SEVEN:
THE ONE MILLON DOLLAR MAN

Whilst it could easily be argued Steve Austin was well worth the Six Million dollars it cost to put him back together, when news broke Nottingham Forest had paid a Million pounds for Birmingham City's Trevor Francis, I, like so many was shocked. A Million pound for a footballer? The world had gone mad but who was anyone to argue with Brian Clough and Peter Taylor? Francis was a fantastic talent, lightning fast, explosive, a deadly finisher, if anyone why not him? Whether he would ever be able to beat Steve Austin in a race or pull Lindsay Wagner remained dubious, although come the European Cup Final later that season, Trevor Francis did score the winning goal. But, Lindsay?

On Saturday 24th February, after two weeks of FA Cup football, Manchester United returned to First Division action against Aston Villa at Old Trafford and quite literally stunk the place out. They achieved a double, booed off at half and full-time, as the 44,337 crowd let rip. Villa were no better, but they had little need to be. A Jimmy Greenhoff penalty gave United a share of the points in a 1-1 draw, but it was truly rotten stuff, instantly forgettable. (Elsewhere, Liverpool won 6-0 at home to Norwich, with two from Dalglish and Johnson, and one apiece for A Kennedy, and R Kennedy).

Next up for a Manchester United team once more under pressure, another home game. This time to Queens Park Rangers who themselves were fighting desperately against relegation, couldn't buy a point for a quarter of Kop Kops and ultimately proved easy meat for this United that remained stuck in an identity crisis. A sparse crowd by Old Trafford standards of just over 36,000, living proof the fans were sick to the back tooth of Dave Sexton's under-performers, and how they were being sent out to play. Alarm bells again rang out in the United corridor of powers. Seeing swathes of empty seats was

akin to a cannon going off in the boardroom and the whisky vanishing. Sexton needed a lift, but from where? He appeared unwilling to embrace the United attacking football philosophy, and it was swiftly becoming apparent to all that only success in the FA Cup could well save him. Waiting for us in the Quarter Finals was Tottenham Hotspur away at White Hart lane, the tie of the round and one that already had my full attention.
(Elsewhere, Liverpool won 2-0 away at Derby County, with goals from Dalglish and Kennedy).

As March reared its head, Manchester United travelled to Bristol City to earn a hard fought 2-1 win. Showing more on the road, probably down to less pressure from the home fans, it was a fine comeback. After a Gerry Gow goal, (Captain Caveman), put the home side in front, the reds replied with Steve Coppell and Gordon McQueen to seal the points. All eyes now turned to the forthcoming cup match against the Spurs. League games were fine, but by this time they'd become like buying a plain cone off Bertaloni's ice cream van, when you could've had a flake in it with raspberry sauce on for a couple of pennies more. What was the point? All about the FA Cup.
(Elsewhere, Liverpool drew 0-0 away to Chelsea).

ACT TWENTY EIGHT:
THE THIRD MONTH OF 1979

I first saw Osvaldo Ardiles live at Maine Road playing for Tottenham Hotspurs against non-league Altrincham in an FA Cup Third Round replay. The Robins had gone to White Hart Lane putting in a fantastic performance to grab a 1-1 draw, indeed many neutrals claimed they should have won. Spurs survived though and the replay was switched to Maine Road from Moss Lane for capacity reasons. Dad got the tickets and we settled down in Platt Lane. It was an interesting crowd, there were many neutrals, blues and reds obviously supporting Altrincham, but also taking the opportunity to come and see Spur's Argentinian duo who both were expected to play, and did so. Osvaldo Ardiles and Ricardo Villa. That the Londoners won comfortably courtesy of a Colin Lee hat trick wasn't the story for the vast majority of watching punters, including me and dad, who could simply not take our eyes off Ardiles. A slim, frail darting figure in the middle of the park making Altrincham players dance to his will. One time in the centre circle he back-heeled the ball through two opponent's legs, before coming away with it. Another, Ardiles dropped a shoulder and three surrounding Altrincham players ended up back at Moss Lane. This was an Argentinian box of tricks that took your breath away. All around supporters just stood applauding, smiling, marvelling at this little genius who had come to us from another continent. Hardly ever likely, but if football could be compared to ballet then Osvaldo Ardiles was Swan Lake. A truly beautiful footballer.

North London.
Saturday 10th March 1979.
The atmosphere inside White Hart Lane edged towards warlike as kick-off drew near. United's red army had infiltrated all over across the terraces and pockets of fighting were breaking out around the

stadium. In went the police with batons and fist-no nonsense, God help anyone arrested with a Manchester accent in the cells. Spurs fans bombarding with beer cups, coins, cans, anything they can get their hands on towards those reds being led along the touchline towards the official away end. No such thing in the seventies, wherever the red army travelled, chaos, mayhem and carnage duly followed. Turnstiles jumped, roofs scaled. The burning whiff of a simmering fuse, tension so tight it gripped the chest, Police horses lined up resembling a charge of the light brigade and the strong smell of alcohol enough to knock a bear flat on its back. This was Manchester United away in North London,

in the third month of 1979.

51,800 held their breath as the game began. Only three places stood between them. United sixth, Spurs ninth, both vastly underachieving for the amount of talent both possessed. It was to be the home side who dominated the first half. Gary Bailey lucky to be given a foul when he dropped a cross and Chris Jones taking advantage, putting the ball in the net, only for it to be ruled out. United were pushed back constantly-Osvaldo Ardiles, Ricky Villa and Glenn Hoddle buzzed and bossed the midfield, their interplay at times bewildering. Opportunities for the Spurs were many-Hoddle's brilliant free kick finding Don McAllister, whose header smashed against the bar. On twenty-seven minutes they deservedly took the lead when from a Steve Perryman floating free kick, Ardiles nipped in front of a stranded Bailey to plant a cleverly arched header into the net. Three quarters of White Hart exploded! Come half-time it remained 1-0, justifiably so. Manchester United needed badly to raise their game, and following the interval they at last came into the contest. Firstly Steve Coppell bursting through only to mishit at the last-Jimmy Greenhoff with a ferocious effort into the side-netting. Coppell once more, a flashing header stopped brilliantly by the keeper Mark Kendall diving to push the ball away. Such pressure had to show and an equaliser for United arrived on the hour with a first goal for Mickey Thomas. Sammy McIlroy's low corner was met by an in-rushing Thomas, and after an accidental one-two off Gordon

McQueen's leg, the little Welsh winger bundled the ball home, before celebrating in front of jubilant United supporters. Sensing blood, the reds attacked once more with Ritchie only inches away when his header from Jimmy Greenhoff's cross brushed the crossbar. It was breathtaking stuff! On came Joe Jordan to replace the youngster, this being big Joe's first game back since getting injured playing for Scotland against Portugal in November. It continued, Gordon McQueen flattened Chris Jones in the penalty area and as the Spurs player and fans raged what was undoubtedly a foul, the referee waved play on. The other end, Steve Perryman's horribly misplaced back pass was intercepted by the speeding Coppell, whose cross flew across the six-yard box before being cleared-Spurs sub Peter Taylor took on the entire United defence before lashing a shot inches of Bailey's post. The clock ran down, still both teams looked for a winner and in the dying moments Sammy McIlroy ran clear, his shot cleared off the goal line, rebounding to Ashley Grimes who blasted well over. The final whistle, 1-1, a classic FA Cup encounter leaving all who played and watched it breathless. A replay in four days' time at Old Trafford lay in wait. United had once more albeit, belatedly turned up in the FA Cup. Long may it continue.
(Elsewhere, Liverpool won 1-0 away at holders Ipswich Town with a goal from Dalglish to advance into the Semi Final).

The following Monday afternoon was the draw for the FA Cup Semi-Finals. There was of course a one in four chance (even my Maths had that sussed), we could get them, if, if, the reds beat Spurs in the replay. Then, it happened, the balls came out and suddenly Wembley appeared half a world, not just a country away. No doubt the draw would fire up United's players and fans more than ever now to send those North London cockneys home with nothing more than a programme the coming Wednesday evening under the Old Trafford floodlights. The prize for such was Liverpool in the Semi-Finals at Maine Road. This enough to focus a twelve-year-old's mind on his school lessons for once and keep my mind occupied. Sod it, in for a penny: "What was that about Stalagtites Mr Kulakowski?"

Wednesday 14th March 1979. A huge 55,584 crowd turned up to ensure Manchester United would have the backing from the terraces. The main team news was Andy Ritchie dropping back down to the bench as a fit again Joe Jordan returned to start, and as ever for a game of such magnitude at Old Trafford, with the stakes so high, a special atmosphere engulfed the stadium. In a sparkling first-half display the reds simply ran the legs off a Spurs side almost unrecognisable in terms of performance from their Saturday efforts. The reds took a deserved lead when from a Sammy McIlroy free-kick, the much missed Jordan rose high at the fire post to plant a fine header past Mark Kendall. From that moment there was little doubt, but it wasn't until midway through the second-half when McIlroy cleverly finished off Micky Thomas' run and cross in front of the Streford End, that United and the fans could truly breathe easy. As the game drifted from that point towards its inevitable conclusion, thoughts, well mine anyway turned to what lay ahead in the next round. The huge cheer at the final whistle from across the terraces saluting and cheering Dave Sexton's men off the pitch-a rarity itself those days, came with the realisation that if the dream of a third Cup Final in four years was to be achieved then our greatest rival down the East Lancs road had to be overcome. Manchester United rose to such a challenge back in 1977, a game truly defining the beginning of a rivalry that now had grown into a crescendo of hatred. The reds ruined their treble bid, the animosity grew way out of control, pure venom and vitriol-the Munich chants became a despised favourite from the Liverpool song book. That on the field Bob Paisley's men on the day had no equals as shown on Boxing Day at Old Trafford, it was also true they could be beaten. This was a United team that came alive in the FA Cup and whilst neither rhyme nor reason could explain, it gave us a chance in the mad, beautiful game I loved.
(Elsewhere, Liverpool drew 1-1 away at Everton, with a goal by Dalglish).

ACT TWENTY NINE:
SHOOTING STAR

Rushing, late for school as always.
Flying out the door, bag hanging off my shoulders, the garden gate left swinging. Running at full pelt round to Moston Lane, then, crossing without looking and within an inch of getting knocked over and killed by a milk float. I kid you not. What a description to put on your gravestone. "Never the fastest, but getting run over by a milk float?" At first I thought I had got away with it, just a terse "Watch where you're going you dozy little idiot!" off the milkman. Only to discover to my absolute horror an entire busload of Saint Matthew kids had witnessed my unfortunate incident whilst it stood stationary at the Ben Brierley bus stop. Not my finest moment and there were many milk-related jokes handed out that day.

Leading up to the Liverpool Semi Final, Manchester United played three League games which all but summed up the season. Firstly, Coventry away at Highfield Road on a Wednesday evening when in a mad dash of a contest, the reds finally lost 4-3, after one time being dismantle 4-1. A first defeat in eight games. Two goals down after only eight minutes we grabbed one back through Steve Coppell, but right on half time that fine Scottish winger Tommy Hutchinson made it 3-1. (Later to sign for Manchester City and complicate my young teenage years even more with his brilliance). A fourth was added by defender Bobby Macdonald, (also City bound) shortly after the restart to surely finish United off, but not so. Sammy McIlroy made it 4-2, a mere consolation, only for then Coppell to strike again late on setting up a dramatic finale. Alas, it wasn't to be, and this loss to Gordon Milne's team saw the reds drop to ninth place.
(Elsewhere, Liverpool won 2-0 at home to Wolves with goals from Dalglish and McDermott).

Four days later in what had become typical schizophrenic manner, on Saturday 24th March 1979, Manchester United destroyed Leeds, our great rivals from the wrong side of the Pennines, 4-1. The highlight being a sensational hat trick from Andy Ritchie, who only knew he was playing shortly before kick-off when Joe Jordan pulled out. It was a stunning performance from the Manchester teenager. A perfect three, a left foot, right foot and a header. The 51,191 loving every touch of this tall, mobile kid with a deadly eye for goal armed with great technique, and showing signs of already having that rare air around him of being a "Proper" United player. Within the opening twenty-minutes the reds were three up, two from Ritchie including a great right-footed strike, a header and another from the non-stop Mickey Thomas, who himself was getting better with every game played. Leeds pulled one back through Ray Hankin in the second, but the result was never in doubt and with ten minutes remaining, Ritchie completed his hat trick with a thunderous left-footed shot in front of the Stretford End. 4-1, and the reds in decent enough form for what lay ahead. It appeared a lengthy career at United was in the making for Andy Ritchie, but such is football it wouldn't be at Old Trafford. In what turned out to be a bittersweet, if wonderfully short adventure for a lad raised United red, Ritchie went on to score a total of thirteen goals before being moved on by Dave Sexton in 1980, for £500,000 to Brighton & Hove Albion. Sadly, Andy Ritchie was to be just a shooting star. Shipped out in order to help part-finance the transfer for Nottingham Forest's Gary Birtles. Much to the anger of Manchester United supporters, but what did we know?
(Elsewhere, Liverpool won 2-0 at home against Ipswich Town with goals from Dalglish and Johnson).

Four days before the Maine Road showdown, Manchester United travelled to the North East, Middlesbrough's Ayresome Park, and as had become their party piece, the reds only started to play when 2-0 down. After being blitzed by Boro in the first-half with goals from David Armstrong and Mark Proctor, it could have been so many more, the reds finally woke up to force a 2-2 draw. Firstly, Steve

Coppell just after the break to begin an onslaught that ended with Gordon McQueen marauding forward to snatch a late, if deserved equaliser. So, I'm sure it's become quite apparent that all roads in this story have inevitably led to this finale. I just hope you've enjoyed the journey arriving here. "Come with me now," said Rod Serling at the being of each Twilight Zone episode. "You're traveling through another dimension, a dimension not only of sight and sound, but of mind. A journey into a wondrous land, whose boundaries are that of imagination. That's the signpost up ahead - your next stop." Manchester United v Liverpool in the 1979 FA Cup Semi Final.

ACT THIRTY:
A SIMPLE BLOODY FOOTBALL MATCH

Saturday 31st March 1979.
  Looking for stuff to kill in the hours before the forthcoming, tumultuous afternoon's clash against the dark side, I pottered around our garden dribbling the ball about and firing it against the fence several times, before the obligatory shout and Mum's head popping out from the kitchen: "John, stop kicking the ball at the fence! Go and play with it on the front!" Not a clever idea for when this nervous about a United game, I was far better off on my own. I wasn't in the mood for chit chat with a neighbour or God forbid a mate turning up at the gate, especially a blue one. No, I kicked the ball away and headed upstairs to my bedroom. It was time for the Subbuteo tactics session which I perfected many years before Andy Gray tried claiming it on SkySports. Sadly, no matter how hard I tried moving figures around all led to us getting hammered later on. I even played the match beforehand with a totally neutral head and United still got beat 4-0. Clearly not doing myself any favours, I gave up and set off to watch Grandstand's Football Focus downstairs. It was just gone Twelve o'clock. Frank Bough gave way to Bob Wilson and as the talk turned to the Semi-Final and of Liverpool being by far the better team?-this was torture, what the hell was I going to be like when old enough to go to the games on my own? (I was terrible by the way). Maybe music was the answer, so I searched out one of my few albums, the rest was Mum's, she had loads and found my Dean Freidman album. "Well Well Said the Rocking Chair." I really liked Dean-and another band I was hearing more of on the radio, called The Jam. No good, there remained only one option left, to go and fetch my ball and have a walk around to the croft. There under the grand shadow of Saint Dunstan's church, I could hammer away the frustrations by smashing it against a wall, each time ridding the

Liverpool demons from my head, one to eleven. Far too young for drugs and alcohol, what else was I supposed to do? I was a strange kid.

 With Three o'clock almost upon them the two teams emerged from the respective Maine Road dressing rooms. Many appeared tense with their game faces already set, a few jovial. Emlyn Hughes beaming wide chatting away to Martin Buchan, who I hoped was just being polite as the rival Captain. Across the Maine Road terraces the torrent of hatred between the supporters was hard to underplay. It was vile and dangerous, the violence and hooliganism menacingly additive for many of both colours-able to go from hurling insult to bricks and coins in an instance. A clash of great Northern cities, their proud clubs, come 1979, sliced apart by a Stanley knife. Since the 1977 FA Cup final, it had become so much more than simple rivalry, poisoned by the course of the region's history, the building of the Manchester Ship Canal crippling Liverpool shipping, the sick Munich chants, the bitterness. Although there had been dislike between the two before the 77 Final, there remained a modicum of respect between older supporters, afterwards even that thinned out.
 Rows and rows of the thin blue line, many actually itching for a fight. The Manchester constabulary, a fair few with dogs straining to be let loose. All stood in lines watching the crowd, waiting. Each passing moment to kick off the hostility increased ever more. It was a tinder box. Both sides would play in their away strips, United, white shirts, black shorts, Liverpool, an all yellow strip, not the white they wore on Boxing Day, which I took as a good omen. On the teams coming into sight it was an explosion of noise that not only rocked the stadium, the surrounding Moss Side area, but across all South Manchester. It was like a bomb going off. Moody simply not doing it justice. Dave Sexton received a warm greeting from the Liverpool back room staff. Handshakes all around as Manchester United in the white tracksuits top, Liverpool, their yellow kit broke to different ends of the pitch to scenes of utter fanaticism from their supporters. 52,524 ignited into a fervor in this football ground of normal blue persuasion.

THE TEAMS

Manchester United. Bailey, Nicholl, Albiston, McIlroy, McQueen, Buchan, Coppell, J Greenhoff, Jordan, B Greenhoff and Thomas.

Liverpool. Clemence, Neal, Thompson, Hansen, Hughes, Case, McDermott, Souness, Dalglish and Johnson.

 It was United to kick off and the opening seventeen minutes saw us well in the game, comfortable even, then like a cobra Kenny Dalglish came ominously alive inside the penalty area. The white shirts of Buchan and McIlroy twisted one way, then another before Dalglish finally enabled himself room to fire low past a diving Gary Bailey from eight yards. Manic Scouse celebrations broke out, it was a glorious goal, one so typical of this horrible genius that hurt like hell. Already since arriving in the summer of 1977, he'd scored fifty-one goals in just a hundred appearances. Now, the moment for the real Manchester United to show themselves. Would it be the one that fell down like dominoes at Birmingham and was destroyed and embarrassed by Liverpool over Christmas. Or the United that swept Manchester City aside on this very pitch and the team who fought back at the Spurs, before wiping the floor with them in the replay at Old Trafford? Two minutes later as the Liverpool fans were still joyfully singing their goal scorer's name, a high hit and hope lofted cross over his shoulder by Jimmy Greenhoff, into their penalty area was met by a leaping Joe Jordan, whose thumping header flew past Ray Clemence into the bottom corner of the net!1-1! A goal out of nothing but one that meant absolutely everything! Suddenly, the eruption of noise that reverberated across the terraces came with Mancunian accents screaming towards the heavens. The first goal Liverpool had conceded in the season's competition. This wasn't a football match, it was a war-Jordan ran off with arms outstretched, wearing a huge toothless grin. The big Scot embraced by teammates, his partner in crime up front and goal-maker Jimmy Greenhoff, foremost amongst them. Leaping round our front room, almost crying with relief it appeared the Manchester United I'd prayed for had shown up after all. Grow up, you're twelve now my inner sensible self was telling me. Game on! If possible the noise grew to an even higher level of fury, as did the already breathless pace of the contest. Another opportunity shown itself for Dalglish at the far post, as Gary Bailey initially rushed out too quick, but he managed to make amends blocking for a corner. This was an unfortunate trait of the young United keeper, a tendency to come for the ball when it was safer to stay on his line.

Every tackle and challenge was being fought out at breakneck pace. Phil Thompson took out Joe Jordan in the centre circle and was handed a yellow card. His studs scraping down the back of the recently injured Jordan who handed the Liverpool defender a look that would have sent a police dog running for cover. The game continued with Steve Coppell leading the charge attacking down the right hand side, his cross found Jimmy Greenhoff whose snapshot flashed wide-but it was United pushing forward showing no fear. Yet, the danger remained every time Liverpool crossed the half-way line. Jimmy Cases' cross found Kenny Dalglish with his back to goal in the box with Buchan behind him, Dalglish fell to the ground: a penalty! The Liverpool supporters at that same end erupted in delight. The referee gestured for a push, the United players went mad, a raging Gordon McQueen booked, but the decision stood. Up ran Terry McDermott to smash against the left hand post and away! With Maine Road in utter bedlam, the ball was worked back by Liverpool to Graeme Souness, who with time to set up his shot fired in a ferocious drive that Bailey tipped away for a corner! Immediately, the ball was cleared by United to Sammy McIlroy who sped away over the half-way line, only to be finally brought to ground by McDermott. Everybody could at last take a breather...

United hit back, a mishit from Brian Greenhoff on the edge of the box landed at Joe Jordan's feet, twelve yards out, but falling as he took aim, Jordan's low shot was saved by Clemence. Again, the reds had the momentum when McQueen went crashing in on Souness,

before soaring off through a sea of yellow shirts over the half-way line, with the ball at his feet, before finally being dragged back by the normally, ice cool Alan Hansen, who was rightly booked. Big Gordon a sight to behold when in full flow and in the midst of such a thunderous battle even more so. Half-time arrived like a fire engine needing to douse fires and just throw water over a Maine Road crowd that lay gripped with excitement, but also a crippling tension. A game where supporter's heartbeats didn't just flutter they came flying out of chests. Another forty-five minutes of pure unmitigated torture remained, back at Rosslyn Road, I handled the pressure in my own unique style by retreating to the bedroom with my red and white scarf on and pretending it didn't really matter in that wonderous, universal scheme of things. After all imagine you was on the Moon looking back at the Earth who would bother to care about a simple, bloody football match? There were so many more important subjects I could, and should have been getting worked up about, but on that long gone, now early Spring day back in 1979,
I just couldn't think of any.

United began the second-half in similar style pushing Liverpool back. One more than any other in a white shirt excelled, the bundle of energy and whiplash left winger born in Mochdre, Colwyn bay in North Wales, Mickey Thomas. Constantly harassing the yellow shirts, and whenever possibly scurrying into dangerous areas causing Paisley's team endless problems. On fifty-six minutes Jimmy Greenhoff again lifted a high cross into the box wreaking mayhem in front of Clemence-first to it was Coppell slipping the ball off to Brian Greenhoff, who with an astute touch from eight yards out hooked the ball over the stranded keeper into the net! Once more the red army went into raptures. Maine Road rocked, swayed and this creaking old stadium rang out to a deafening cacophony of ''Wembley, Wembley, we're the famous Man United and we're going to Wembley!''
 So much time remained though, enough for Liverpool to still stuff this chant down our necks, for nothing was more certain they would come after us now with everything in their armoury. It was like a

yellow rain falling down in torrents on Gary Bailey's goal with United players snapping, cutting off space, flying into tackles, whilst always with one eye looking to break out. One time the normally master of all ceremonies Graeme Souness was on the ball outside the United box, only to find himself literally mugged by three white shirts. Liverpool were finding ways through though and only a last gasp tackle by Albiston prevented McDermott getting a shot off. A substitution, Jimmy Case for the flying winger Steve Heighway sent Liverpool up yet another gear. Paisley's machine had clicked into full working order. United were holding, just, Jimmy Nicholl and Gordon McQueen both limping, but defending heroically. Suddenly, there remained only fifteen-minutes left to play-Jimmy Greenhoff had possession on the edge of the Liverpool box and was pushed over, a free kick. Up came Sammy McIlroy to run over the ball before Mickey Thomas curled a wonderfully, arching free kick that Clemence saved magnificently tipping over the bar. From the resulting corner McIlroy's precise cross found an unmarked Gordon McQueen who inexplicably from only four yards out flashed his header wide! United players held their heads in hands, was that the chance? Wave after wave of yellow shirts poured forward. Liverpool's football was astonishingly crisp, imaginative, cutting, but ultimately a creaking magnificently, resilient Manchester United rearguard, led as ever by the impeccable Martin Buchan held their line. Finally, such ferocious, intense pressure had to tell and a volleyed McDermott lob found Kenny Dalglish clear with just Bailey to beat and as the Manchester United fans shut their eyes, he for once hopelessly miscued by chipping the ball over the bar. Straight from that United counter attacked and a Jimmy Greenhoff header put Steve Coppell clear on goal, only to fire past Clemence's far post. A horrified Coppell fell to his knees. An opportunity to wrap the game up had gone and Sexton's men, brave as they had been were tempting all echelons of footballing fate, especially against a team like Liverpool. The songs from the red army grew louder, especially when Joe Jordan put Jimmy Greenhoff clear on goal, only for Clemence to come charging out and clear. Back came Liverpool, Steve Heighway wreaked havoc to set up Ray Kennedy on the six-yard box, only to be thwarted from a certain equaliser by the courageous Bailey diving at his feet. It was exhilarating and thrilling but devastating for Mancunian hearts, especially mine with Liverpool now encamped outside the United penalty area. By this time there was no way out, a siege. They came again, a Dalglish overhead cross caused havoc, a Johnson downward header found Souness, who turned and shot past Bailey, only for Martin Buchan to clear off the goal line out for a corner-this was cleared by United, but only to Phil Neal. Crossing the half-way line, Neal fed McDermott, who in turn played in Steve Heighway. Seven minutes remained, off sped the lightning Heighway to flash in a low cross that Bailey couldn't hold, the ball fell loose and waiting to pounce from six yards was Liverpool centre half Alan Hansen. 2-2! Off soared Hansen back down the pitch with arms raised to take the salute of a jubilant, but so relieved Liverpool support. United appeared spent, on their knees. It had been a truly, heroic effort, but ultimately they'd been worn down and now with their tails up Liverpool would surely try and finish United off without the need of a replay. A fantastic cross- field pass from McDermott set Heighway clear on the left facing Arthur Albiston. The winger cut inside letting fly a powerful low drive from twenty-yards that Bailey saved brilliantly at his near post. Time almost up. The dying embers of the game consisted of Liverpool looking desperately for a winner, but the bloodied but unyielding United defence kicked and headed away everything thrown at them in the penalty area. It was ironic that the referee's final whistle blew with Gordon McQueen in mid-air clearing yet another cross. A standing ovation for both teams followed. Feelings remained high in the tunnel afterwards with Emlyn Hughes shouting out for all to hear: ''You Mancs have had your chance, we'll do you on Wednesday!'' Only to receive off a nearby big Gordon a smack in the mouth for such disrespect. Players of both sides stepped in and a stunned Hughes was led back to the Liverpool dressing room not sure what day it was. It had been a monumental effort from United, just seven minutes away from a glorious victory, but now we'd have to do it all again. This time twenty-eight miles

away on enemy territory. Everton's, Goodison Park. At least when it came to support there would be an even split inside the ground come Wednesday night. Proud, battered and unbowed. Manchester United remained in the FA Cup, but the general consensus appeared to be the reds had blown it, a feeling widely felt by even many of our own supporters. Queuing at Gill's Newsagents for Dad's Football Pink later that evening, this was definitely the opinion of all present. An hour on from the game, I'd had chance to calm down a little. After Alan Hansen's late equaliser, I think I experienced my first end of the world moment, but once having time to think how close we had come to knocking them out? The dejection turned to renewed hope, for United had proved they could go toe to toe with one of the world's great teams. There remained in me the dreamer, the hopeless football romantic thinking maybe, just maybe we might have their measure. At Maine Road that day Joe Jordan and Jimmy Greenhoff had tormented the normally, flawless, unflappable Phil Thompson and Alan Hansen. Jimmy especially was the scourge of Anfield with his recent form of breaking Liverpool hearts. Who was to say given the opportunity at Goodison Park,
 Jimmy couldn't do so again?

ACT THIRTY ONE:
ON THE RADIO

Wednesday 4th April 1979.
It had been a tiring, weary day in school. My mind twenty-eight miles away on Merseyside planning tactics to beat Liverpool and go on to play Arsenal in the FA Cup Final. Come that final bell resonating loud, (always like a starting pistol for me) I was out of that gate faster than a British Leyland striker. Dad had got lucky that same day with a ticket for Goodison and would be heading straight over after work with his mate, Pete Cassidy. £1.20 each! Me, I set up in the front room downstairs and would at least have someone to share the pain. Nan was coming around to have her hair put in rollers by mum, and afterwards the usual sorting the world to rights. This meant no chance was she going back home leaving me alone to go through hell dealing with the match on the radio. Obviously though after Coronation Street. (The one where Stan tells Eddie to get the hens moved, fearing Hilda's reaction). Nan never watched or listened to United for her nerves simply couldn't stand it. She'd iron, wash, cook, paint, sweep the yard, anything to take her mind off the football, but once over she'd be straight on the phone to me. It was a ritual we had for thirty-years and even now when the full time whistle blows on a United game goes, I'm waiting for her call that never comes. Back then though my nan sat across the table as we shared on the radio, what remains for me today despite all the riches since my most memorable night supporting the reds.

Once home and changed out of school uniform, I was sat watching John Craven's News round, but always with one eye on the clock. Nationwide, The Wonderful World of Disney, suddenly, it was gone Seven o'clock. Mum and nan were in the kitchen, I switched on BBC Radio Two for their full second-half commentary with Alan Parry, the wonderful Peter Jones and expert analysis from the one and only King of the Stretford End himself. Denis Law. If all went well BBC1 Sportsnight at 9-35, to watch the match, if not, bed. Hopefully, please God, Saint Dunstan, Pope John Paul 11 and all the angels and saints in heaven, I'll see you later Mr Carpenter.

As at Maine Road on Saturday,
  Manchester United were in white shirts and black shorts, Liverpool, all yellow. As for team changes, one each with Lou Macari replacing the injured Brian Greenhoff and Steve Heighway starting for Jimmy Case. With the United supporters filling half of Goodison, their heartbeat became the old, wooden Park End behind the goal, for one evening transformed into the Stretford End. If possible, the noise inside the stadium surpassed even Saturday. During the seventies, the travelling red army experienced many an occasion that would be claimed at the time as utterly unsurpassable, but nothing came close to what occurred at Goodison Park. Nothing. It was a show of support so raw and impassioned. That night the red army terrace classic Scarlet Ribbon was born, the song like the evening set to enter Manchester United legend. United began on fire attacking the Liverpool end and putting Liverpool immediately on the back foot. Joe Jordan finding Sammy McIlroy, whose deft touch set up Lou Macari to charge inside the penalty area and fire in a low drive, well saved by Ray Clemence. As the ball rolled clear first to it was Jordan, who again found McIlroy, fifteen yards out, only for Sammy to screw his shot horribly wide of Clemence's goal. Arguments were breaking out already amongst the Liverpool players to wake up. Terry McDermott and Graeme Souness demanding concentration as United continued to pour forward. Lou Macari, Sammy McIlroy and Mickey Thomas were dominating in midfield and a long ball hammered forward by Macari troubled Phil Thompson, whose header fell straight at Jordan's feet, who ran clear with just Clemence to beat. Out he came to save from the Scotsman and also Steve Coppell following in like a steam train. The Park End roared out: "United!" Liverpool didn't know what was hitting them as Sexton's team had gone off like a rocket, but it couldn't last. Finally, they came alive when Steve

Heighway skipped past Gordon McQueen to reach the goal-line.
Looking up, Heighway pulled back a cross that McDermott killed in
an instance for Souness to lash in a fiercely hit snapshot saved
wonderfully by Gary Bailey low down-protected by a host of white
shirts around him. Manchester United continued to roar forward. A
Sammy McIlroy free-kick saw a mad scramble ensue, ending with
Gordon McQueen horribly slashing the ball over from just five yards
out. The popular defender appeared disgusted with himself. McQueen
had missed a similar chance in the first game and his frustration
clearly shown through. Still United threw caution to the wind and
moments later a McIlroy corner was met with a ferocious Jordan
header that smashed violently against the bar! Across the Manchester
United end of the ground and especially the Park End there was
riotous scenes as every man, woman and child stood cheering and
screaming their team on. "We are the pride of all Europe, the cock of
the North!" Through sheer graft and no small amount of tactical nous
and skill, Macari, McIlroy and Thomas were playing and running their
highly accomplished midfield counterparts off the pitch. Yet, despite
such domination nothing to show. This was Liverpool. They'd took a
hiding for thirty-five minutes and it remained scoreless. The Scouser's
years of European experience, of going away to foreign climes,
receiving a chasing, but ultimately coming through with a result. Soak
up the pressure, kill the opponent's legs and then strike. A rare foray
forward saw Phil Neal launch a cross and running from deep with no
white shirts picking him up was Ray Kennedy. He took aim with a
thumping header that flew past Bailey only to smash against the bar!
Suddenly, the Gladys End of the ground where the vast majority of
the Liverpool fans were roared out! A dose of reality. A moment if
needed to remind all in love with Manchester United just who we
were up against.
 Half-time arrived,
  and the Semi Final replay remained God knows how scoreless! I was
a wreck. For the second-half nan was joining me in my torture.
Coronation Street was over, Stan Ogden was in big trouble with Hilda
once more and life now could continue as normal. Mum decided to do

some cleaning, just as well for what she knew about football, I could write on a chewit. Not nan though, I was worried she might not be able to handle the stress, and yet there was me, Mr cool with no fingernails, a nervous wreck and a hot line to the heavens praying for divine intervention.

Alan Parry began the first part of the second-half radio commentary telling us Ray Clemence had played in eighteen Semi-Finals for Liverpool, and never lost. "Well its about time he did then," said nan, clearly not impressed. The match went on, Martin Buchan cleared from Kenny Dalglish in what had been a great battle between the two- Phil Neal got off a shot saved easy by Bailey. Parry advise us to watch the match later on Sportsnight, easy for him to say. The analyser Denis law started to talk and nan thought she recognised his voice, 'Is that Denis law?"

I nod

'Is he still playing?" added mum. "Must be getting on a bit." It was the sort of comment not really needed in this time of great anxiety. 'No mum, he's retired, he retired years ago. Denis is commentating." Clemence came off his line to run into a brick wall called Joe Jordan. 'Get up," said nan, shaking her head. It was far more Liverpool now. In what would prove to be Emlyn Hughes's last game for Liverpool, he played a ball forward for Dalglish who was worryingly being mentioned more often. Liverpool were starting to take control. It was frightening stuff. I looked up and there was mum happily dusting down the mantlepiece and humming. Humming?! What's wrong with people who don't love football? Impressive as United had been in the first-half denied only by the brilliant Clemence, it had become clear this was now a totally different Semi Final. A score was announced elsewhere. "West Bromwich Albion 3 Manchester City 0."

'Some good news," I said to nan, who nodded in agreement. In his first game back after six weeks, Lou Macari had run, fought and whenever the chance arose tried also to get forward. Lou, Sammy McIlroy and Mickey Thomas did appear though to be starting to run on empty. This not helped when Souness took out Thomas with a shocking tackle. Nan was off her chair: "He should be in jail him, not

on a bloody football pitch!" It was all Liverpool-Johnson let in
Heighway, but McQueen cleared for a corner. Foremost amongst the
scheming yellow shirts was of course Dalglish weaving his magic-
though nothing really was being created. "Liverpool are now starting
to show their authority," piped up Denis Law. The Lawman's
comment not doing much for our state of mind. Elsewhere, another
score flash. "Nottingham Forest 3 Aston Villa 0" and the One Million
Dollar man Trever Francis had got two. Money well spent it appeared.
A huge roar of disapproval erupted from the radio, you could almost
hear the Mancunian accents roar in derision as Emlyn Hughes took
out Steve Coppell with a knee high tackle and receive a deserved
yellow card. Hughes was obviously still touchy from being laid out in
the Maine Road tunnel on Saturday by Gordon McQueen. This had us
both up standing: "That bleeding Emlyn Hughes!" snarled nan.
"Never trust anyone who smiles all the time John, they've got
something to hide." I nodded; she wasn't wrong about much! David
Johnson worked hard to let Dalglish in, but was foiled by Gary Bailey
being swift off his line. Though I tried so hard not think about it I felt
a sense of inevitability that they were going to score-our midfield was
being over-run. Johnson again with a wonderful pass was met first
time by an unmarked Graeme Souness, who thankfully shot way over
the bar. As Parry spoke of Martin Buchan holding United together at
the back, mum started to dust down the radiogram behind me, still
humming. I was starting to think I wish I could be like her, obviously
mum wanted us to win, but it definitely wasn't life or death. My point
proved as she started to sing quietly: "Too much, Too little, Too late"
by Johnny Mathis and Denice Williams.
Oh, not to care so much!

Coppell went down in the Liverpool area after another reckless
challenge by Hughes, but no penalty. Heighway broke out at full pace,
only to smash into Lou Macari, as Lou's 'They (the yellow shirts)
shalt not pass attitude was displayed in all its beauty. Twenty minutes
into the second half-Ray Kennedy fired a right footed rocket way over
the bar after being set up by Phil Thomas. Bailey again off his line
fast before Dalglish could get a shot off. It was tense, tight and
traumatic and equally so at 30 Rosslyn Road. "One goal will surely

be enough," commented Parry. The ferocious pace of the first-half had dropped and this far suited Liverpool more. A breather for United when a Macari break out earned a corner and an opportunity to catch breath. The time came for a change of commentator and for the last twenty two and a half minutes of this epic contest entered the one and only Peter Jones. His opening line: 'So, the battle of the red roses still rages then!' Absolutely wonderful!

All Liverpool pressure-Arthur Albiston put the ball behind for a corner that Heighway took and McQueen belted away. The end felt nigh as Jones' voice went up a notch describing Kenny Dalglish in our penalty box. Liverpool were so much better, Dalglish again with his back to goal, only for Buchan to put the ball behind for yet another corner down at the Gladys End. Too many corners, far too many. Another great duel had been Alan Hansen and Joe Jordan. The footballing centre-half against an old fashioned, ferocious Centre-forward. Yellow shirts buzzing around, the ball moving now fast, looking for holes. The Liverpool machine was starting to grind Manchester United into the turf, yet still Macari, McIlroy and Thomas attempted to hunt them down. Buchan and McQueen remained solid behind, Dalglish getting desperate now threw himself to the floor after a Macari challenge, no penalty-it went on. David Johnson played in Souness, whose wild shot flew harmlessly over the bar. Jones commented on scuffles breaking out around him in the stand. There would be so much worse later outside the ground. "What happens if it's a draw?" asked Mum. "Do they both go to Wembley." I glared across as she dusted down her Stylistics album and daren't answer, I simply tutted in disgust. United had the ball, nan looked at the clock, then to mum. "I hope your Dad doesn't forget his key Maureen; he'll be off out now for the last hour in the Ben Brierley. Like bloody clockwork!"

Suddenly, though, United had the ball.

Let Peter Jones describe what happened next.

"Bailey plays it straight into the Liverpool half...A challenge from Jordan...Breaks to Mickey Thomas...It's the turn of Liverpool to challenge...A chance here for Jimmy Greenhoff...Jimmy Greenhoff has scored for Manchester United!...Oh, what a goal!...The man who scored the winning goal in the 1977 FA Cup final when United beat Liverpool 2-1...The man who scored in every round except the Quarter Final...The man who said he wanted to score in every round, including Wembley...Well, Jimmy Greenhoff with a most beautiful header...Lovely work by Mickey Thomas...Greenhoff was there, Clemence did everything he could, it wasn't enough...Jimmy Greenhoff with the header, and could that goal be taking Manchester United back to Wembley?!''

On seventy-seven minutes, Sammy McIlroy had swept forward into the Liverpool half, his pass finding Mickey Thomas, whose low, sweet left-wing cross was met by Jimmy Greenhoff to stoop low and finally beat Ray Clemence with a gloriously, placed header into his far corner, igniting scenes of euphoria and riotous celebrations in the Park End and across Goodison Park! Those in the Park End were convinced the stand was crumbling as it bounced and shook! Suddenly, the full extent of just how many Manchester United supporters were present in the stadium became apparent. They were all over the place! After being mobbed by jubilant teammates, Greenhoff found himself alone for a moment with his striking partner Joe Jordan and proceeded to plant a kiss on his cheek. It was a beautiful relationship!

As Peter Jones described the goal, me and nan were up hugging, going crazy! Even mum joined in! She knew, she just knew! None of us would be sitting down again! Thirteen minutes remained.

''I'll go put the kettle on,'' said Mum, in that kind of English stereotypical manner, you would say if a meteorite was heading towards earth and only had thirteen-minutes before it hit! The game restarted-a substitution, Andy Ritchie for the totally spent Lou Macari, who had given every last drop of energy. Lou's chippy at the top of Sir Matt Busby Way, half decent but never no Golden Apple in its prime! As the United fans sang and danced in utter joy, the yellow shirts of Liverpool flung themselves on the attack. It was no longer controlled football, it had become frenetic, To be beaten by the bitterest rivals at the home of Everton, their Merseyside neighbours would prove such a bitter pill to swallow, as to almost choke them. McDermott to Kennedy who set up Souness, but he couldn't get a shot away from the edge of the box. It was a white and black wall! Still, Liverpool swarmed all over the United goal. Heighway sped clear only to be tackled by the substitute Ritchie, straight away in the thick of the action. Ten minutes remained; Emlyn Hughes flung a hopeful free-kick forward that was cleared to set Joe Jordan chasing after it. Behind Jordan the beseeching voices of 25,000 Manchester United supporters, urging him on! Already amongst the red hordes chants of "Wembley!" were becoming louder and more hopeful. Oh God, fate made you pay for tempting it with sweet whisperings. Again, through the radio Peter Jones' voice rose a decibel as Liverpool were in our penalty area. "The ball is bouncing around a clatter of players. The shot comes in! Wide!" That rare magic of Jones' ability to paint pictures in your head came with both beautiful and horrifying consequences. It was torturous, unforgettable, football poetry. The clocked ticked ever further down, McDermott was off for Jimmy Case. It was like swapping one huge moustache for another. Five minutes to survive: Ray Kennedy let fly from twenty-five yards, but his effort was blocked down as whites shirts rushed towards him- Dalglish moved in trying to find room for a shot, but he too was crowded out. Three minutes…Whistles already from the Manchester United end, a deafening crescendo. Souness on the half-way line, probing and pushing yellow shirts forward. His long ball headed clear by Gordon McQueen for yet another corner-Case swung it in and Joe Jordan slammed it clear for Sammy McIlroy, who was simply far too weary to chase. Ray Clemence kicked the ball deep back into the United half and guess who, McQueen once more headed it away. Kennedy picked up and found Johnson, his hopeful shot from twenty-yards was blocked by Coppell. A minute and ten seconds: a throw in for Liverpool-Neal passed back to Clemence to hoof forward and Arthur Albiston was there to concede a throw-in, midway inside

the United half. Alan Hansen sprung over the half-way line, the ball
with Graeme Souness still trying so hard to find a hole in the United
defence, but there was simply none to see. Maybe, for the last time
Souness moved forward only to be stopped in his tracks by Jimmy
Nicholl...

The final whistle, and to quote the great man Peter Jones:
"Manchester United are going back to Wembley!"

Across the pitch and in the United end of Goodison, wild, emotional
scenes broke out. "Wembley, Wembley, we're the famous Man
United and we're going to Wembley!" The United fans sang this from
the rooftops as the sound of stomping feet whilst doing so was heard
for miles around! Somehow, Dave Sexton's much maligned at times,
but on their day formidable opposition for anyone had pulled off a
remarkable result. On the touchline a typically, reserved Sexton was
sportingly congratulated by Liverpool manager Bill Paisley and
members of their Boot Room, Ronnie Moran and Joe Fagin.

Elsewhere, in the stand a joyful Brian Greenhoff was sat near Peter
Jones and he joined him for a quick chat saying: "Oh, it's fantastic
honestly, and I'm very pleased my brother got a great goal against
them this time!"

Later, outside the ground utter mayhem ensued between the two sets
of supporters and few coaches headed back down the East Lancs with
all their windows intact. For Manchester United supporters it was the
sweetest of victories in Liverpool's backyard, but the hatred and
bitterness that had been brewing between them since the 1977 FA Cup
final, exploded in truly extraordinary scenes of violence outside
Goodison Park. Due to the Semi Final ticket distribution, there were
thousands more United fans present than would be normally at a
League match between the two and scenes of football hooliganism,
rarely seen in this country up to that time, (even the notorious red
army of the mid-seventies adventures), turned the surrounding streets
of Goodison into a battle ground. The sound of police sirens echoed
well into the Merseyside night. Total and utter chaos, carnage.

"Have you got the time mate?" A line used by Liverpool fans to trick
Mancunians into answering and then...

Back at 30 Rosslyn Road, the final whistle was greeted with cheers, no little relief, tears, (mine mostly) and hugs. Big hugs! "The last time I listen to that lot" said nan and she never did so again! Nan found any excuse possible not to, but come the final whistle at every Manchester United game for the next thirty years or more the phone would go and I filled her in on what went on! Or, If I had been to the game, I would ring nan. Mum took a call off a delighted Dad. The message for me, whatever I did, make sure I didn't miss the match on the telly and he'd tell me all about it later! I looked at the clock, almost time for Sportsnight.

Well, hello there Mr Carpenter! We've only gone and bloody done it! One important task to complete though before John Motson's dulcet tones. Out came the MUFC OK notepad and with great care I logged the night's result. This the only time of that season I added the goalscorer's name and the venue.

Manchester United 1 Liverpool 0. J Greenhoff. Goodison Park!

POST MATCH

It's hard to believe this all happened forty four years ago. The magic of that long one evening has never left me. Since, Manchester United have gone on to achieve unbelievable success winning a dazzling array of trophies. League titles, European cups, we've been blessed with countless, magnificent games and players. Unforgettable occasions. "If I hadn't seen such riches" sang Tim Booth. No one has enjoyed such times more than me, but, if pushed when asked for my favourite United moment, I always refer back to Goodison Park 1979. As a young boy United was a first love. My first girlfriend didn't come along until two seasons (years) later! A fortnight in Torquay and whilst there we lost 1-0 to Wolves away. Many people in this story are no longer around, except in my heart. Nan and grandad have passed away. Captain Jackie also. Peter Jones, Dave Sexton, Brian Greenhoff...RIP all. This ultimately has been about a Manchester lad obsessed by football and more so Manchester United It has been the tale of a very special night for me that I shared with people I loved a long time ago now.
Way back in 79,
on the Radio.

MANCHESTER UNITED LEAGUE AND CUP FIXTURES 1978-79

19 August 1978: Birmingham City H: 1–0: Jordan: 56,139

23 August 1978: Leeds United: A: 3–2: Macari, McIlroy, McQueen: 36,845

26 August 1978: Ipswich Town: A: 0–3: 21,802

2 September 1978: Everton: H: 1–1:Buchan: 53,982

9 September 1978: Queens Park Rangers: A: 1–1 J. Greenhoff: 23,477

16 September 1978: Nottingham Forest: H: 1–1 J. Greenhoff: 53,039

23 September 1978: Arsenal: A: 1–1: Coppell: 45,393

30 September 1978: Manchester City: H:1–0: Jordan: 55,301

7 October 1978: Middlesbrough: H: 3–2: Macari (2), Jordan: 45,402

14 October 1978:Aston Villa : A : 2–2 : Macari, McIlroy, 36,204

21 October 1978: Bristol City: H: 1–3: J. Greenhoff: 47,211

28 October 1978: **Wolverhampton Wanderers A: 4–2: J. Greenhoff (2), B. Greenhoff, Jordan: 23,141**

4 November 1978: **Southampton: H: 1–1: J. Greenhoff: 46,259**

11 November 1978: **Birmingham City: A: 1–5: Jordan: 23,550**

18 November 1978: **Ipswich Town: H: 2–0: Coppell, J. Greenhoff: 42,109**

21 November 1978: **Everton: A: 0–3: 42,126**

25 November 1978: **Chelsea: A: 1–0: J. Greenhoff: 28,162**

9 December 1978: **Derby County: A: 3–1: Ritchie (2), J. Greenhoff: 23,180**

16 December 1978: **Tottenham Hotspur: H: 2–0: McIlroy, Ritchie: 52,026**

22 December 1978: **Bolton Wanderers: A: 0–3: 32,390**

26 December 1978: **Liverpool: H: 0–3: 54,910**

30 December 1978: **West Bromwich Albion: H: 3–5 B. Greenhoff, McIlroy, McQueen: 45,091**

3 February 1979: **Arsenal: H: 0–2: 45,460**

10 February 1979: **Manchester City: A: 3–0 Coppell (2), Ritchie: 46,151**

24 February 1979: Aston Villa: H: 1–1: J. Greenhoff: 44,437

28 February 1979: Queens Park Rangers: H: 2–0: Coppell, J. Greenhoff 36,085

3 March 1979: Bristol City: A: 2–1: McQueen, Ritchie: 24,583

20 March 1979: Coventry City: A: 3–4: Coppell (2), McIlroy: 25,382

24 March 1979: Leeds United: H: 4–1: Ritchie (3), Thomas: 51,191

27 March 1979: Middlesbrough: A: 2–2: Coppell, McQueen: 20,138

7 April 1979: Norwich City: A: 2–2: Macari, McQueen, 19,382

11 April 1979: Bolton Wanderers: H: 1–2: Buchan: 49,617

14 April 1979: Liverpool: A: 0–2: 46,608

16 April 1979: Coventry City: H: 0–0: 43,035

18 April 1979: Nottingham Forest: A: 1–1: Jordan: 33,074

21 April 1979: Tottenham Hotspur:A: 1–1: McQueen: 36,665

25 April 1979: Norwich City: H: 1–0: Macari: 33,678

28 April 1979: **Derby County: H: 0–0: 42,546**

30 April 1979: **Southampton: A: 1–1: Ritchie: 21,616**

5 May 1979: **West Bromwich Albion: A: 0–1: 27,960**

7 May 1979: **Wolverhampton Wanderers: H: 3–2: Coppell (2), Ritchie: 39,402**

16 May 1979: **Chelsea: H: 1–1: Coppell: 38,109**

FA Cup

15 January 1979: **Round 3: Chelsea: H: 3–0: Coppell, J. Greenhoff, Grimes: 38,743**

31 January 1979: **Round 4: Fulham: A: 1–1: J. Greenhoff: 25,229**

12 February 1979: **Round 4: Replay: Fulham: H: 1–0: J. Greenhoff: 41,200**

20 February 1979: **Round 5: Colchester United: A: 1–0: J. Greenhoff: 13,171**

10 March 1979: **Round 6: Tottenham Hotspur: A: 1–1: Thomas: 51,800**

14 March 1979: **Round 6: Replay: Tottenham Hotspur: H: 2–0: McIlroy, Jordan: 55,584**

31 March 1979: **Semi-Final: Liverpool: Maine Road: 2–2: Jordan, B. Greenhoff: 52,524**

4 April 1979: **Semi-Final Replay: Liverpool: Goodison Park: 1–0: J. Greenhoff: 53,069**

12 May 1979: **Final: Arsenal: Wembley: 2–3: McQueen, McIlroy: 100,000**

League Cup

30 August 1978: **Round 2: Stockport County: H: 3–2 McIlroy, J. Greenhoff, Jordan: 41,761**

4 October 1978: **Round 3: Watford: H: 1–2: Jordan: 40,534**

THE END

Printed in Great Britain
by Amazon

36249670R00069